WECK
Small-Batch
Preserving

WECK

Small-Batch Preserving

YEAR-ROUND RECIPES FOR CANNING, FERMENTING, PICKLING, AND MORE

STEPHANIE THUROW

Skyhorse Publishing

Copyright © 2018 by Stephanie Thurow
Photography © 2018 by Stephanie Thurow

Skyhorse Publishing books may be purchased in bulk at special discounts for sales promotion, corporate gifts, fund-raising, or educational purposes. Special editions can also be created to specifications. For details, contact the Special Sales Department, Skyhorse Publishing, 307 West 36th Street, 11th Floor, New York, NY 10018 or info@skyhorsepublishing.com.

Skyhorse® and Skyhorse Publishing® are registered trademarks of Skyhorse Publishing, Inc.®, a Delaware corporation.

Visit our website at www.skyhorsepublishing.com.

10 9 8 7 6 5 4

Library of Congress Cataloging-in-Publication Data is available on file.

Cover design by Jenny Zemanek and Mona Lin
Cover photo by Stephanie Thurow

Print ISBN: 978-1-5107-3562-0
Ebook ISBN: 978-1-5107-3563-7

Printed in China

For Ben

Thank you for your unwavering support and love behind all that I do.

CONTENTS

INTRODUCTION

My affinity for WECK jars began after my friend introduced me to them in 2008. I had never seen anything like them before. The ones she had were small, lovely glass jars with glass lids and a rubber ring with two metal clamps. We were a little nervous to try canning with them for the first time, but we quickly learned there was nothing to fear. After our first experience canning with WECK jars, I started a collection of my own, which eventually turned into an obsession. I've even been called a hoarder a time or two regarding my WECK jar collection, but I'm okay with that—actually, even proud to be.

I nannied for my baby cousin throughout my college years, and after reading books on infants and becoming more informed about children overall, I became aware of all the toxins and harmful chemicals surrounding us in our daily lives, so I started to rid plastic from my own household. Years later when my own daughter was born, I was in a full-on war with plastic, BPA (Bisphenol A), phthalates, PVC, and other potentially harmful items around my house. This meant that the regular canning jars I had been using up to this point were also off limits due to the BPA-lined jar lids. That's when I switched over to using strictly WECK jars for my home canning. I didn't want any toxins leaching into my organic canned goods! In 2012, the FDA banned the use of BPA in infant-related products (baby bottles, formula liner, etc.) and many other brands started moving away from the use of BPA in their products as well, often advertising them as "BPA-free." Though it gave me a sense of comfort, I always wondered what "safer alternative" they were using in place of BPA. *Was it indeed safer?* I once again began incorporating the other jars and lids back into my home-canning routine until I read a study published by UCLA in 2016 stating that "BPA-free alternatives may be no safer than BPA." (Read the study online at academic.oup.com/endo/article/157/2/636/2422708.) So, with the best interest of my family in mind, I've recently made the switch back to water-bath canning strictly with WECK jars for my personal use. I'm sticking with the "better safe than sorry" idiom. Because WECK jars and their lids are made of glass, the only material touching the preserve is glass, so I do not have to worry about any harmful chemicals leaching into my food, and that gives me peace of mind. Plus, the lids are reusable, so I don't need to purchase new lids after each use and that is a great bonus. This means less waste, which translates to eco-friendliness!

When the J. Weck Company chose to collaborate with *me* to write a preserving guide, it was a dream come true. If I'm not their biggest fan, I'm definitely one of their top five! Throughout this book, I share more than one hundred small-batch water-bath canned, fermented, pickled, and infused recipes, all designed for WECK jars. The recipes are written in an easy-to-read format that a novice can understand and an experienced preservationist can appreciate. Preserving in small batches is a fantastic way to try out a recipe without investing too much time, money, or energy. Small-batch recipes equal less preparation time, less cost for the ingredients, and less storage space required. If you love a particular recipe, double or triple it! I've included a handful of fantastic guest recipe contributions throughout the book with tips from industry pros, as well as note sections paired with each recipe for you to jot down what you liked about the recipe, what you didn't like, what you changed, what worked, what didn't, etc. I want you to use my recipes as a jumping-off point for future creations as you gain confidence in food preservation. I hope this book puts you at ease about how to use these aesthetically beautiful, non-toxic, and versatile jars, and I hope you find this cookbook to be inspirational and educational as it guides you through your food preservation endeavors. Happy Preserving!

Stephanie

PART I

THE HISTORY OF WECK® JARS

A chemist named Dr. Rudolf Rempel discovered that food could be successfully preserved by heating it in glass jars with an abraded edge, rubber ring, and metal lid. His discovery was patented in 1892, but he died in 1893. Albert Hussener founded a company which produced glass jars, but the company was not successful, probably because of the lack of advertising for his new product. He sold the patent to Johann Weck.

Johann Weck was born near Frankfurt, Germany. He moved to the town of Öflingen, in the state of Baden, as soon as he had bought Rempel's patent. Weck was a strict vegetarian and an abstainer from alcohol. With his products he wanted to fight against the disease of alcoholism which was very common at the time. The surroundings in southern Baden were rich in fruit trees and fulfilled his wishes of preserving fruit instead of using it to make alcohol. He had acquired the exclusive right for distribution of the newly patented glass jars and canning apparatus for the entire area of southern Germany. He also bought the sole proprietorship of the company and the WECK canning patent.

He realized very soon that he could not manage the whole project alone. He found a partner from Lower Rhine area who was the local sales distributor for WECK products. The businessman, Georg van Eyck, was operating a porcelain and pottery shop. Around 1895, he took up the offer of Joann Weck to sell home canning jars. Georg van Eyck sold more canning jars in his shop alone than were sold in all other shops in Germany. Van Eyck had a special commercial talent, and he realized that he had to introduce his customers to the practical side of food preservation. When Weck asked him how he succeeded in selling so many jars, he also asked him if he would come to Öflingen to take over the sales of WECK products for all of Germany. Van Eyck agreed and founded together with Johann Weck the J. Weck Company on January 1, 1900.

With foresight and energy Georg van Eyck built up the company in Germany and the neighboring countries of Austria, Belgium, France, Hungary, Luxembourg, the Netherlands, and Switzerland. He did not become discouraged when Johann Weck decided to leave the firm in 1902 for personal reasons. Van Eyck built up his own staff and organized introductory sales shows for the whole country, just as he had done at his own shop. He employed teachers of domestic science who gave practical advice and instructions at cooking classes, parishes, and hospitals. He constantly improved his products: the jars, rubber sealing, canners, thermometers, and all the accessories which were sold under the trademark of WECK. With the trademark WECK, Georg van Eyck created one of the first trademarks in Germany, and also used advanced strategies of advertising by introducing the trademark name written across a red strawberry, which is still a well-known German label today.

Both world wars resulted in big setbacks for the WECK Company. When World War I started, all foreign trade contracts with the European countries and Russia came to a halt. In World War II, the three WECK glass factories that were located in the East were confiscated without damages being paid.

The WECK glass factory near Bonn—still under the ownership of the grandchildren of its founder Georg van Eyck—took up production after the war, in 1950. It has developed into a very modern, almost fully automated glass factory which today produces not only home canning jars but also bottles for soft drinks, jars and commercially preserved foods. The WECK Company has also produced a home and garden magazine *Ratgeber Frau und Familie* ("Advisor – Woman and Family") for more than one hundred seventeen years. This monthly magazine is read in more than one million German-speaking households. The headquarters of the J. WECK Company are still in Öflingen, Germany.

ABOUT WECK® JARS

WECK jars are gorgeous tempered-glass jars that come in a variety of shapes and sizes. Each jar has a distinctive orange rubber ring, a glass lid, and two rust-proof stainless-steel clamps that securely close the jar. The metal clamps fit all WECK jars, and the jar lids and rubber rings of different styles fit interchangeably on jars of the same size. The rubber ring aids in sealing the jars so that the only material exposed to the preserves is glass, making WECK jars completely non-toxic. WECK jars are European and therefore do not translate exactly over to American sizing of half pint, pint, and quart jars. However, WECK jars are very similar in size. Here's a list of the styles of jars I most commonly use for preserving.

all jars

cylindrical jars

Cylindrical jars are ideal for both canning and fermenting. The tall, thin design of jar model numbers 905 and 908 make them perfect for asparagus pickles. The smaller cylindrical jars (905) are great for infusions, and the larger jars (908 and 974) are fantastic for ferments such as kimchi or sauerkraut.

deco jars

Deco jars are beautifully shaped and ideal for canning jams, sauces, and small-batch ferments. They are also great for decorative purposes and dried food storage.

juice jars

Juice jars of all sizes are the perfect jars to use for infusions. The neck of the jar helps keep the infused ingredients submerged. The smaller juice jar (763) is ideal for completed shrubs, infusions, or kvass.

Mold jars are most commonly used in my home kitchen. They are perfect for both ferments and canned goods. The largest jar of the collection (743) is my preferred jar of choice for making kvass. The 742 can be used equally in canning and fermenting as it is closest to a pint-sized jar. The 740 is great for jams, chutneys, and other "jam jar" sized preserves.

mold jars

Tulip jars are shapely and gorgeous once filled with fruits and veggies. The smallest two of the collection (762 and 744) are ideal for jams, chutneys, and sauces. The 745 is a perfect quart jar option for canning and fermenting.

tulip jars

Mini mold jars are so adorable. It's surprising all the ways you'll find to fill them! I use the smallest of the collection (080) for organizing my salts and seasonings. I also store homemade ground horseradish (pg. 68) in them.

mini mold jars

WECK® jars closest to an 8 fl. oz. jam jar

Jar Style	Style #	Size (Liters)	Fluid Ounces
Deco Jar	902	⅕ L	7.4 fl. oz.
Mold Jar	740	⅕ L	9.8 fl. oz.
Mold Jar	900 (tall)	⅕ L	9.8 fl. oz.
Tulip	762	⅕ L	7.4 fl. oz.

WECK® jars closest to a 16 fl. oz. pint jar

Jar Style	Style #	Size (Liters)	Fluid Ounces
Deco Jar	901	½ L	18.9 fl. oz.
Mold Jar	741	¼ L	12.5 fl. oz.
Mold Jar	742	½ L	19.6 fl. oz.
Tulip Jar	744	½ L	19.6 fl. oz.

WECK® jars closest to a 32 fl. oz. quart jar

Jar Style	Style #	Size (Liters)	Fluid Ounces
Cylindrical Jar	908	1 L	35.2 fl. oz.
Deco Jar	748	1 L	35.9 fl. oz.
Mold Jar	743	¾ L	28.7 fl. oz.
Tulip Jar	745	1 L	35.9 fl. oz.

WECK jars have not been tested by the USDA for home canning, therefore are not "approved" by the USDA for home canning, but this does not mean they are not safe for home canning. They have been safely used in home and commercial canning in Europe and around the world since 1900. The recipes in this book have been designed for WECK jars specifically, though measurements can be converted to fit standard 8-ounce, 16-ounce, and 32-ounce home canning jars that are USDA-approved. Please keep in mind that the headspace recommended per recipe will vary from ½ to ¼ inches if using any jar other than a WECK jar. Water-bath canned recipes from other cookbooks can be converted to fit WECK jars in a relatively similar size by adjusting the headspace to ½ inch.

CANNING AND FERMENTING: EXPLAINING THE DIFFERENCES

If you've read my first book, *Can It & Ferment It*, parts of the next few sections may be a bit of a repeat, though I encourage you to keep reading as bits and pieces vary and are tailored to WECK jars.

Water-Bath Canning

The process of water-bath canning allows us to preserve food with freshness and at peak flavor. This method of preservation creates an airtight environment in which bacteria and other harmful contaminates cannot survive after going through the high-heat process of the boiling water bath. Through this preservation process, acidic canned goods become shelf stable and can be stored in a pantry or cupboard for one to two years. They can keep for more than one year, but for the best flavor, texture, nutrients, and taste, try to keep to the twelve- to eighteen-month timeframe, as it all begins to deplete once preserved.

Fermenting

Fermented recipes in this book are foods that are fermented in salt or a saltwater brine (salt dissolved in water). The process of fermentation can take days, weeks, months, or even years depending on the flavor desired and the specific fruit or vegetable used (though the recipes in this book generally take only a few days or weeks). The process of vegetable fermentation creates an acidic environment (by converting sugar into acid) in which bad/unsafe bacteria cannot survive. This is known as lactic acid fermentation or more popularly termed, "lacto-fermentation" or "wild-fermentation." Lactic acid preserves the texture, taste, and nutrients in fermented foods. Lacto-fermented foods create probiotics, the healthy gut bacteria. The studies on fermented foods are endless and truly fascinating to read. If you haven't already, I encourage you to take some time to research the health benefits linked to fermented foods. See the resource section in the back of the book for reading recommendations (pg. 178).

Importance of Local and Organic Produce

Can and ferment with the freshest available fruits and vegetables whenever possible; they are going to have the best flavor if they are picked at their peak and also retain more nutritional value compared to produce from the grocery store. Most of the produce sold at the grocery store is picked long before it's ripe, and by the time it reaches the store shelves it's lost much of its vitamins and nutrients. Per the USDA National Institute of Food and Agriculture, produce that is canned promptly after harvest can be more nutritious than fresh produce sold in local stores. The USDA goes on to say that within one to two weeks, even refrigerated produce loses half or more of some of its vitamins. I recommend buying produce at the farmers' market that has been harvested the day of or the day prior, that way the produce is preserved within twenty-four to forty-eight hours of when it's harvested. Use organic produce whenever possible and always use produce that is not treated with a food-grade wax sealant or harsh chemicals. Wash all produce before using.

In addition to using freshly harvested foods, when selecting produce be sure to pick fruits and vegetables that are not bruised or damaged. I also recommend trying to select produce that's uniform in size. Having uniformity allows the food to pickle or ferment evenly which will result in a consistent end product.

Farmers are happy to explain their farming practices. By talking to local farmers, I have discovered that many fruits and veggies are indeed farmed organically, but the farmers have not gone through the process of making that official due to the cost incurred. Do not hesitate to ask your farmer questions about the way they farm—you might be pleasantly surprised by their answers. Be sure to always ask when the produce was harvested to ensure freshness.

CANNING INGREDIENTS AND SUPPLIES

Salt: canning salt, also known as pickling salt, is preferred for water-bath canning; it is pure sodium chloride. Kosher salt is also acceptable, though the amounts may vary. Be sure to check a salt conversion chart. You can find one at: mortonsalt.com/article/salt-conversion-chart/. Never use iodized salt.

Vinegar: only use vinegars that indicate a 5–6 percent acidity level. Many bottles will note "pickling vinegar" on the packaging. I've personally only used store-bought vinegar because it offers reliable acidity results and I know it's safe. For the sake of simplicity, every recipe in this cookbook will call for 5 percent acidity, distilled white vinegar, or organic apple cider vinegar.

Sugar: as you've probably noticed, canned jams, jellies, chutneys, and other sweet preserves generally include more granulated sugar than you'd expect. Sugar helps not only preserve the color, but also helps the canned goods gel and become firm instead of syrup-like. Ohio State University Extension Services states that sugar also acts as a preservative by inhibiting microbial activity; thus, recipes should not be modified or adapted. Brown sugar and honey can be substituted for granulated sugar in recipes, though it will not cut down the overall carbohydrate content. It is not promoted by the Extension Services to use artificial sweeteners when canning preserves. (Read more online at extension.oregonstate.edu/lane/sites/default/files/images/sp50303.pdf.) There are liquid and powder pectin options on the market that will help reduce sugar in recipes, though none of the recipes in this book call for it. If you purchase pectin to reduce sugar in these recipes, please be sure to read the directions that come with the pectin packaging to fully understand how to use it. Pectin can be found online or in the canning section of most supermarkets.

Water: the purest water you have available to you is the best option. I have a reverse osmosis system at home that I often use. Water with minerals such as iron could cause discoloration but is fine to use. I've canned with tap water for many years and it's worked great with the water from the city where I live. Some chemicals added to city water could possibly cause an adverse reaction to the end-product, but you may need to learn by trial and error to know if your tap water will work. If you are in a rural area and have well water as your main source, you can have the water tested to see if there has been any contamination. If you are unsure, store-bought water is an option.

Lemon juice: a couple of recipes in this book call for lemon juice. Use fresh juice from lemons or store-bought lemon juice but know that it is recommended by the USDA to use store-bought lemon juice when canning, since the acidity level is reliable when compared to using fresh lemons.

Common Canning Supplies

- Large water-bath canning pot with lid and a rack, 21–33 quarts in size. These are typically sold in big-box stores in a starter set or online. The rack is required to keep the jars off the bottom of the pot and allows water to flow around all sides of the jars. Canning pots range from about $20 to $100. Read the range recommendations for each water-bath canner; some do not work with electric, glass-top ranges.

- Stainless-steel wide-mouth funnel.
- WECK jars in a variety of sizes and styles, including the rubber rings and metal clamps they come with.
- WECK jar canning tongs/jar lifter to insert and remove jars from the hot water bath.
- Stainless-steel potato masher, used when making jam.
- Stainless-steel ladle.
- Variety of 1-, 2-, 4-, and 8-cup measuring cups.
- Measuring spoons in a variety of sizes.
- Clean lint-free towels or paper towels.
- Sharp paring knife.
- Stainless-steel butter knife, used to remove air pockets from hot and cold packed jars.
- Large- and medium-sized thick bottomed, non-reactive (stainless-steel or enamel-lined) pots for making jams, sauces, and brines.
- Candy thermometer, to measure the temperature of the water or jam sauce (not required for any of the recipes in the book, but convenient to have on hand when canning or if you want to test the temperature to be on the safe side).
- Occasionally throughout the book, a food processor, fine mesh strainer, mandolin slicer, apple peeler, or hand blender would streamline the process in some recipes. These are not required for canning but very helpful to have on hand when needed.

The USDA recommends using plastic utensils when canning; however, I personally only use stainless steel, as I do not like to heat plastic. I've never had a jar break due to using stainless steel, but if you are leery, feel free to use plastic funnels, ladles, and other utensils.

CANNING WITH WECK®

Food Safety Recommendations

Jars filled with raw-packed food must be processed in warmer water and slowly heated (versus a boiling bath), to allow the contents to gradually heat up and avoid breakage. Make sure the water-bath canner is hot but not simmering, then submerge all jars in the water bath, cover the water-bath pot with the lid, and increase temperature so the contents of the jar can safely heat. Once the canner has reached a boil, start the timer per your recipe instructions.

Due to food safety recommendations in America, the orange rubber rings on WECK jars should be replaced after each water bath, though in Europe (where the jars have been used for home canning for more than one hundred years) the rubber rings are reused multiple times until they stretch, crack, or break. I've been canning with WECK jars for more than a decade and I've always reused the rings without a problem. However, if the rubber ring is cracked, over-stretched, or broken do not use it for home canning. To inspect rubber rings for flaws before processing, hold the ring between your thumb and forefinger with both hands and tug lightly while turning the ring clockwise. WECK rubber rings are perfectly safe to reuse over and over for fermentation, but use your judgement when deciding whether to replace or reuse the ring each time it's used for water-bath canning.

Hot Pack versus Cold Pack

There are two main ways to fill jars when canning. The hot pack method is when a jar is filled with hot, precooked food such as jam. The cold pack a.k.a. raw pack method is when a jar is filled with uncooked produce and the fruit or veggies are covered with a hot liquid brine or syrup. The liquid needs to be hot during this process; otherwise, there is a risk of the jar breaking during the water-bath process. A jar breaking during processing will occasionally happen (even to the best of us) and unfortunately all contents of the broken or cracked jar must be carefully disposed of and cannot be reused. Both methods of hot and cold packing result in sealing the jars via the boiling hot water-bath method. It's important to always leave headspace in the jars between the top of the liquid or food and rim of the jar. When canning with other jars, the recipes vary from ¼ to ½ inches of headspace for water-bath canned recipes, but because this cookbook is designed for WECK jars, all water-bath canned recipes will require the same ½ inch of headspace per the WECK Company's recommendation. This extra space allows for expansion of the food in the jar during the sealing process. When packing jars with fruits or veggies in preparation for the hot water bath, it's important to try and remove any air bubbles trapped within the contents of the jar to reduce the risk of spoilage. I use a stainless-steel chopstick to aid in removing bubbles when packing hot and cold packs, but a stainless-steel butter knife works just as well.

The Process of Boiling

Water-bath canning involves submerging filled jars into a hot water bath. This process kills bacteria that might otherwise cause spoilage and creates a vacuum that removes air from jars and seals them tightly to prevent any outside contamination. This process allows for long-term storage without refrigeration.

When canning, always be sure to check the rims of the jars and lids to make sure there are no cracks or chips. Do not use jars with defects or they will not properly seal. Per the USDA, jars filled with high-acid preserves that are water-bath canned ten minutes or longer do not require sterilization. Every canning recipe in this book will be processed ten minutes or longer but I urge you to wash all canning jars with hot water and soap and rinse thoroughly before use. I use a dishwasher to clean my jars, rings, and lids at the same time and I leave them in the dishwasher so they keep warm until I'm ready to fill them.

If you do not have a dishwasher, heat your jars after washing them to keep them warm before filling them. The National Center for Home Preservation recommends submerging jars in hot water, right-side up in the water-bath canner, with water one inch above the jars. Turn the heat up once submerged and allow the jars to simmer until you are ready to fill them with food. Use canning tongs to carefully remove the jars from the water, cautiously dump out the hot water back into the water-bath canner, and carefully set the jars on a clean towel and allow them to cool slightly. Use a small to medium saucepan (depending on lid/ring size you are using) to gently simmer the WECK lids and rubber rings until they are ready to be used, then set them out on a clean towel or napkin for quick access right before use. Jars need to remain warm until they are ready to be filled. Doing so will help avoid breakage of the jars from what is called "thermal shock," which can occur when there is a drastic temperature difference.

Fill water-bath canner with water and bring to a boil. This water will never touch the contents of your preserves. Starting the water-bath canner is one of the first steps I take when canning because it can take a long time for it to reach a boil. The size of jars being sealed will determine how much water to add to the canning pot. If using small jars, the pot only needs to be filled up about halfway (depending on the height of the rack). Keep in mind that once the jars are added to the pot, the water line will rise. You want the water to cover the submerged jars by about one inch when you begin the boiling-water-bath processing time.

Once you're ready to fill jars with fruit/veggies always leave ½ inch of headspace, use a stainless-steel butter knife or other nonreactive tool to remove any air bubbles trapped within the produce and jar (if needed). Next, use a slightly dampened lint-free towel or paper towel to clean the rim of the jar. Remove any traces of food or liquid and wipe again with a dry paper towel to clean the lip of the jar. Place the orange rubber ring and lid on the jar and clip the metal clamps on directly across from one another. The jar and its contents will be hot, so you may need to grip the jar with a towel when adding the metal clamps so you do not burn yourself. It is recommended to read the instructions that come with WECK jars if you have never canned before. Once the water bath is ready, use the jar lifter/canning tongs to carefully transfer the jars into the hot water bath; make sure to keep the jars level.

Sea level plays a factor in how long jars will boil in the water bath. All recipes in this book are based on processing at an elevation of 1,000 feet above sea level or below. See chart and add time to each recipe as needed.

Sea Level	Processing Time
1,001–3,000 ft.	Add 5 minutes to the processing time
3,001–6,000 ft.	Add 10 minutes to the processing time
6,001+ ft.	Add 15 minutes to the processing time

Once the processing time ends, turn the heat to low and let the boiling water settle down for a minute or two. Then, use the jar lifter/canning tongs to carefully lift the jars out of the hot water bath and transfer the jars to a towel-covered counter or table where they will not be disturbed for twelve or more hours. After twelve hours, remove the metal clamps from the jars and test each jar to make sure it is sealed. To test the seal of the jar, simply try to remove the lid from the jar. If it easily lifts off, it has not sealed. The lid should be securely fastened to the jar to have a successful seal. If a jar does not seal after twelve hours, you can keep it in the refrigerator and use within a couple of weeks. Never eat anything that does not look or smell right. Like my grandpa always says, "When in doubt, throw it out!"

Store sealed canned goods in a dark, dry, and cool place. It is not recommended to stack your canned goods. We have an old well in our home that the previous owners covered and built wall shelves on to store canned goods. It's the perfect spot to keep my sealed preserves; organized, dark, and cool. If you don't have a basement or a space like this, put them on the bottom shelf of a cupboard. Refrain from storing the jars up high, as heat rises. According to the USDA, it is best to store your goods between 50 and 70°F. You do not want to display them in a location where they get direct sunlight. Sunlight can cause the color, texture, and flavor of your preserves to change, and it can also deplete nutrients from canned goods. Refrigerate all canned goods after breaking the seal. Fruit-based preserves will last about two months after opening and vinegar-based preserves are best consumed within six months.

Each recipe in this book has a estimated yield amount. The amount per recipe can vary due to the size of fruits or vegetables used. I recommend preparing one or two extra jars in case a recipe makes more than the suggested yield amount. Jars not full enough to be water-bath sealed can be cooled and stored in the refrigerator in an airtight container, but because the preserve did not go through the process of food sterilization from the boiling water bath, it will not last as long in the fridge and will need to be eaten within a couple of weeks (fruit-based preserves) or months (pickles).

CANNING WITH WECK® STEP-BY-STEP

Before canning with WECK jars, inspect the lids and jars for cracks or chips. Should the sealing rim of a jar or sealing portion of the lid be chipped/damaged, recycle it as it will not permit an airtight seal, or reserve it for fermentation use only. All jars should be cleaned with hot, soapy water or run through the dishwasher before use.

1.

Keep jars, lids, and rings warm in either the dishwasher or warm water until use. When ready to can, carefully empty hot water from jars or take a warm jar straight from the dishwasher.

2b.

Fill jars, leaving ½ inch of headspace.

2a.

Use a funnel to safely transfer the hot brine/preserve into each jar.

3.

Wipe the rim of the jar with a clean, dampened, lint-free cloth or paper towel, then again with a dry towel.

4.

Place the rubber ring on the lid. Place the lid with ring on the rim of the jar.

6.

Use canning tongs to carefully place jars into the water bath. Jars should be completely submerged in water. To avoid breakage, the temperature of the water bath should be similar to the temperature of the canned food you are dipping in the water. WECK jars can touch one another or the canning pot wall while processing but they should not be tipped or wedged in. You can stack WECK jars during the water-bath canning process but they need to have an additional rack in between the levels to let the water circulate around all the jars. Once all jars are in the water, cover the water-bath canner with the lid and increase the temperature. Once the water bath begins to boil, set the timer per recipe instructions.

5.

Use the two metal clamps to secure the lid on the jar. Holding with two hands, carefully hook the clamp on the top lid of the jar first, then press firmly until it clicks under the rim of the jar. Still holding the jar, clip the other clamp on directly across from the other. Use a towel if needed to hold jar in place while clipping on the clamps so you do not burn your fingers if the jar contents are hot.

7.

Once processed, turn off the heat and allow the water bath to settle, then carefully remove hot jars from the water-bath canner using canning tongs. I recommend holding a dishtowel under the jar to transfer hot jars from the water bath to the counter or table. Do not tilt jars when removing from the water bath; keep them level. There may be some water caught on the lid of the jars but that is fine, it will evaporate. Allow the jars to cool on a towel-covered surface for twelve hours or more per recipe instructions. Do not remove clamps or touch the jars until they have completely cooled.

8.

Once cooled, the tab on the orange rubber ring should be pointing down; this is an indication that the jar has properly sealed. Remove the clamps and try the "lid-lifting test" by using your fingers to try to gently pull the lid off the base of the jar. The lid should be securely attached to the jar and if so, you have successfully sealed the preserve! It is a fail-safe way to know for certain that your preserve has properly sealed. If the lid does not properly seal, store the preserve in the refrigerator and eat within a couple of weeks.

9.

To open a sealed jar, remove clamps and use two hands to carefully hold the jar and lid in place while pulling the tab on the orange rubber ring outward. You'll hear the suction break and the lid will remove easily. Once the seal is broken, the jar must be securely closed with the ring, lid, and metal clamps and stored in the refrigerator.

Before storing your jars, you should label them with the contents and date. If nothing else, just the date so you can keep track of when it was made. Paint pens are convenient and washable. Custom jar labels are unique and cute, especially for gift giving. You can also use a piece of painter's tape and a permanent marker. I always tell myself I'll remember what I made and when I made it, but after years of forgetting, I've learned that labeling is necessary and helpful.

FERMENTATION INGREDIENTS AND SUPPLIES

Before fermenting, run your supplies through the dishwasher or hand wash them with soapy warm water. No need to sanitize tools or vessels when fermenting. Wooden fermenting supplies generally don't require soap. Read instructions that come with the particular product to learn proper care techniques.

Salt: for the purpose of simplicity, every recipe in this book calls for kosher salt. Sea salt is a great option for fermenting, but the amounts vary due to the fine grain of sea salt. Refer to a salt conversion chart when using alternate salt options. Do not use iodized table salt because it is not pure salt.

Water: the purest water you have available to you is the best option. I have a reverse osmosis system at home from which I use water quite often. Water with minerals such as iron could cause discoloration but typically works great. I've fermented with tap water for many years and it's always been successful with the water from the city where I live. Some chemicals added to city water could possibly cause an adverse reaction to the end product, but you may need to learn by trial and error to know if your tap water will work. If you are in a rural area and have well water as your main source, you can have the water tested to see if there has been any contamination. If you are unsure, store-bought water is also an option.

Common Fermentation Supplies

- Selection of 1-, 2-, 4- and 8-cup measuring cups.
- Measuring spoons in a variety of sizes.
- Stainless-steel wide-mouth funnel for filling jars with fermented foods.
- Clean lint-free towels or paper towels.
- Sharp knife.
- WECK jars in a variety of sizes, typically pint and quart sizes.
- Cutting board.
- Cabbage shredder: optional but helpful.
- Wooden kraut pounder/masher/damper: optional but helpful.
- Food processor to occasionally help streamline a recipe, but not required.
- Weights: lids from smaller WECK jars are excellent weights for fermenting. Even though they aren't super heavy, they usually do a fabulous job of keeping the produce under the brine. Sometimes two lids are needed.

FERMENTING WITH WECK®

Researchers have suggested a link between gut bacteria and the rest of the body's overall health, so not only is fermented food delicious, it's healthy! (Read more online at health.harvard.edu/staying-healthy/can-gut-bacteria-improve-your-health.) Fermented foods are generally made at room temperature, and salt is often used to control the spoilage. Because the fermentation process already starts to break down the food, it's easier for the body to digest as well. The process of fermentation also creates a tangy and sour flavor that cannot be mimicked.

The Fermentation Process

Brine is the liquid added to a ferment (salt dissolved in water) or the liquid that is naturally created by adding salt to a vegetable (such as sauerkraut). Brine level plays a crucial role in the success of a ferment. The brine always needs to cover the fruit/vegetable that is fermenting by about ¼ to 1 inch of headspace. This keeps the ferment from being exposed to air and prevents mold from forming. Low brine level is the main reason ferments go bad, so be adamant about checking the brine level daily.

Headspace is the amount of room between the fermenting food or brine and the rim/lid of the jar. Every fermented recipe requires 1 to 2 inches of headspace because as the produce ferments, carbon dioxide is released, producing small bubbles that can cause the fermenting food to rise in the jar. It's important to check on your ferments every day or two to push the ferment back down and keep the brine level over the produce.

Remove floaters. If you notice small pieces of fruit or vegetable floating up to the surface and hanging out on the top of your brine, use a clean stainless-steel or wooden spoon to scoop out the floater. Floaters make the ferment more susceptible to molding if left in, but if the ferment is a short ferment of 3 days or less, you should not have to worry about them.

Temperature plays a big role in fermentation. As noted in all the fermented recipes in this book, 60 to 75°F (15 to 23°C) is the ideal range for proper fermentation. But keep in mind that the warmer the room is, the quicker fermentation will happen; and conversely, the colder a room is, the slower the fruit or vegetable will ferment. I try to keep my house between 68 and 72°F (20 to 22°C) year-round, as this is the hot-spot range for ferments in my experience. If you do not have air conditioning in the summer, consider leaving a covered ferment in the basement (if you have one) or a cool corner of your home. Otherwise, plan to do most of your fermenting during the cooler months of the year. You could always ask to keep your ferments at a friend's house; I've done it!

Check on your ferments at least once a day for short-duration fermented recipes and every couple of days for long-duration ferments. Check in on them to make sure the brine remains over the fruit/vegetables. Some recipes throughout the book require "burping" a ferment which needs to be done daily or multiple times throughout the day. When checking on ferments, you are also looking to make sure no mold or yeast is developing.

Burping the ferment is required in many recipes throughout the book. During the process of fermentation, carbon dioxide is produced and needs to be released to avoid gas build-up and jar breakage. To burp a ferment, simply remove the jar lid, use a clean hand or utensil to stir or push down the fermenting produce, and securely cover the ferment again. It's that simple!

Cloudy brine and sediment is completely normal and a good thing! When your ferments start the process of fermentation, the brine color will change from clear to cloudy. When fermenting beets, for example, the brine will turn a deep, dark purple. In many ferments you'll see a white sediment on the fermenting produce, or at the bottom of the jar. This is a normal part of the fermentation process, and a sign that things are fermenting as they should.

Kahm yeast is a white thin, powdery-looking film of yeast that grows on the surface of ferments. It's not harmful but has a strong flavor that most people do not like. If caught early, it's easy to remove by dabbing with a paper towel or scooping out with a spoon. If the yeast is mixed in with the brine, it can cause the taste of the ferment to change. Determine if the kahm yeast has spoiled your ferment by taste testing. The best way to avoid yeast is to check the ferment daily and follow the tips mentioned above.

Tannins are naturally occurring in grape leaves, raspberry leaves, oak leaves, and cherry leaves and, that's what helps keep the fermented pickles crunchy. Freeze a few leaves in order to always have them on hand when needed.

INCLUDE THE CHILDREN!

Create lifelong memories and life skills with the children in your life by including them in the preservation process. Here is a list of tasks that children can do to participate. Little will they know they are learning priceless lessons about food preservation!

Note: Suggested tasks may vary; you are the best judge of your child's capabilities.

Ages 1–3

- Pour measured-out ingredients into jars/pots.
- Rinse off fruits and vegetables.
- Break apart cauliflower florets with hands.
- Taste and smell ingredients and seasonings.

Ages 4–5

- Stir salt into water until dissolved.
- Crank the handle of the apple peeler-corer.
- Using a child-safe serrated knife, children can cut soft fruits and veggies into pieces.
- Use a cherry pitter to pit cherries (very fun!)
- Stir ingredients together.
- Mash fruit with potato masher.
- Peel garlic.
- Mix sauerkraut and salt together.

Age 6+

- Use a real knife to carefully cut vegetables and fruit into uniform size pieces.
- Grate veggies.
- Scrub produce clean of dirt.
- Measure ingredients.
- Read recipes.
- Stir hot ingredients over stove.
- Peel veggies as needed.
- Pack jars for fermenting.

PART II

CANNING RECIPES

APPLE BUTTER

I was always told that to make a successful fruit butter, it needed to be cooked "low and slow." Maybe that's the truth for some fruits but I was determined to develop a quick recipe for apple butter and I did just that! No one will be able to tell if this was cooked for one, ten, or twenty-four hours.

YIELD: **4 WECK** jam jars
(4 cups)

3 lb. (8–9 cups) apples, cored and cubed

¼ tsp. canning salt

2 tbsp. lemon juice

¼ cup organic apple cider vinegar

1 cup water

1 ½ tsp. ground cinnamon

¼ tsp. ground cloves

¼ cup raw honey

¼ cup brown sugar, loosely packed

¼ tsp. vanilla extract (optional)

⅛ tsp. ground allspice (optional)

Add apples, salt, lemon juice, apple cider vinegar, water, and cinnamon to a large heavy-bottomed pot. Mix ingredients together, cover, and bring to medium heat. Keep covered and simmer for 20 minutes, stirring occasionally.

Once apples are soft and can be easily smashed with a spoon or fork, remove from heat and let them cool off for a couple of minutes. Using an immersion hand blender or other blender, purée the apples for 1 to 2 minutes into a smooth and silky consistency; be careful not to splash any hot apple mixture on yourself. Add in ground cloves, honey, brown sugar, and optional ingredients if desired. Use a clean spoon to scoop out a small sample to taste and determine if any additional seasonings are needed. Mix well and return mixture to a simmer, uncovered. Simmer on low for 20 minutes to 1 hour, stirring frequently to avoid burning the apple mixture. The length of time to simmer depends on the type of apple used. Some apples create a nice thick sauce after just 20 minutes, while others take 30 to 60 minutes. Generally, by 30 minutes, most sauces will be thick enough to can. I determine thickness by eyeballing the sauce, but for those that don't quite have an eye for it yet, thickness can be tested like this: Once the apple mixture begins to boil down, take out a small spoonful and put it in a glass or ceramic bowl. Put the bowl in the fridge for a few minutes to cool. Once cooled, turn the bowl on its side; the sauce should not move, or move very little. If your sauce does this, it has reached the correct viscosity and is ready to can.

Ladle the hot fruit mixture into warm prepared jars. Use a funnel to safely transfer the mixture, leaving ¼ inch of headspace. Wipe the rims of the jars with a dampened, clean, lint-free cloth or paper towel and again with a dry towel. Place a glass lid with rubber ring in place over the rim of each jar and carefully clip the two metal clamps on each jar directly across from one another. Process in the water bath for 10 minutes. Carefully remove the jars from the water bath with canning tongs and place them on a towel-covered surface for 12 hours without touching. Remove the metal clamps and test the lids to make sure they have securely sealed onto the jars. Refrigerate after opening.

NOTES

APRICOT-CARDAMOM JAM

This recipe has been contributed by Pam Lillis, a master preserver and certified nutritional health coach based in Connecticut. Pam approaches cooking and coaching as a personal journey. She loves to have fun in the kitchen and believes that canned and preserved foods are truly the convenience foods of our time!

YIELD: **6 WECK jam jars
(6 cups)**

3 lb. apricots, pitted and
   quartered, 6–8 pits reserved

3 cups granulated sugar, organic
   or non-GMO

3 tbsp. lemon juice

1 tbsp. crushed cardamom pods

metal tea infuser or fillable paper
   tea bag

Part 1 (to do the night before):

Wash and prepare apricots, cutting away any damaged or bruised areas on the fruit, reserving the pits. Using a hammer, carefully break open the reserved pits, remove the small center kernel and set aside. In a nonreactive glass or stainless-steel pan or bowl, stir together the apricots, sugar, and lemon juice and mix well. Cover with plastic wrap directly on top of the mixture to prevent discoloration and allow it to macerate in the refrigerator for at least 8 hours or overnight.

Note from Pam: While the maceration process may seem like a lot of work, I find it actually makes it quick and easy once your jam session begins!

Part 2 (to do the day of):

Add the crushed cardamom pods to tea infuser or tea bag with the previously saved apricot kernels. Transfer the macerated fruit and sugar to a large, heavy-bottomed pot and bring to a boil over medium-high heat. Add tea infuser or tea bag to pan. Reduce heat to a gentle simmer and cook for 15 to 20 minutes, stirring often to avoid burning. Test the jam with a frozen spoon; if it coats and sticks to the spoon, remove from heat. If not, cook 2 or 3 minutes more.

Ladle the hot fruit mixture into warm prepared jars. Use a funnel to safely transfer the mixture, leaving ¼ inch of headspace. Wipe the rims of the jars with a dampened, clean, lint-free cloth or paper towel and again with a dry towel. Place a glass lid with rubber ring in place over the rim of each jar and carefully clip the two metal clamps on each jar directly across from one another. Process in the water bath for 10 minutes. Carefully remove the jars from the water bath with canning tongs and place them on a towel-covered surface for 12 hours without touching. Remove clamps and test the lid to make sure it has securely sealed onto each jar. Refrigerate after opening.

NOTES

"I have always thought that apricots and other stone fruits are best grilled, roasted, or stewed; the cooking process brings out the wonderful flavor of these beautiful gems. The cardamom pods and the almond flavor of the apricot kernels set this recipe apart and make it a perfect addition to oatmeal, yogurt, and cheeseboards." —Pam

BLOODY MARY MIX

This classic Bloody Mary mix along with other homemade pickle recipes from this book (pg. 75) make the perfect gift-basket idea for your Bloody-Mary-loving friends. It can be served as-is or can be jazzed up with some spice and additional freshly ground horseradish (pg. 68).

YIELD: **3 WECK pint jars (6 cups)**

8 cups ripe tomatoes (5 lbs.), cored and quartered

7 garlic cloves, halved

2 tbsp. onion powder

1 tsp. celery salt

⅛ tsp. ground clove

1 tsp. canning salt

1 tbsp. Worcestershire sauce

1 tsp. ground horseradish (optional)

1 tbsp. lemon juice per jar

If you decide to preserve in WECK quart-sizes jars instead of WECK pint-sized jars, adjust the recipe to include 2 tbsp. of lemon juice per quart jar and water-bath process for 40 minutes.

Wash tomatoes and remove stems and cores as well as any bruised or flawed areas. In a large nonreactive pot, bring all ingredients except the horseradish and lemon juice to a simmer. Simmer 15 to 20 minutes or longer if needed, until the tomatoes have begun to break down.

Remove from heat and use an immersion hand blender to purée the mixture. Then, working in batches, use a fine mesh strainer with a bowl or large measuring cup underneath to separate the juice from the pulp. Use a spatula or spoon to help speed the process along by pushing and stirring the pulp in the strainer and forcing out the liquid. Pour the reserved tomato juice into a large nonreactive sauce pan, add the horseradish if desired (it will lose spiciness as it's cooked), and bring to a boil. Reduce heat and simmer for 3 minutes.

Add 1 tbsp. of lemon juice to each 2-cup WECK jar. Ladle the tomato juice into warm prepared jars. Use a funnel to safely transfer the mixture, leaving ¼ inch of headspace. Wipe the rims of the jars with a dampened, clean, lint-free cloth or paper towel and again with a dry towel. Place a glass lid with rubber ring in place over the rim of each jar and carefully clip the two metal clamps on each jar directly across from one another. Process in the water bath for 35 minutes. Carefully remove the jars from the water bath with canning tongs and place them on a towel-covered surface for 24 hours without touching. Remove clamps and test the lid to make sure it has securely sealed onto each jar. Refrigerate after opening; drink within 1 week of opening.

NOTES

SPICY BLUEBERRY JAM

If you find yourself with excess blueberries this season, preserve a couple jars of this blueberry jam with a kick. Its dark, vibrant color is a stunning contrast spread over goat cheese. Just be sure to label your jar properly so you don't accidentally send your child to school with a peanut butter and spicy blueberry jam sandwich. (Yeah, we totally did that. Oops!)

YIELD: **4 WECK** jam jars (4 cups)

2 lb. fresh blueberries (6 cups)

3 cups organic or non-GMO granulated sugar

2 tbsp. lemon juice

3 tsp. red pepper flakes, add more for more spice

Wash berries and remove stems and soft or damaged berries. Add berries to a large pot and use a potato masher to break them down a bit. Add in the sugar, lemon juice, and red pepper flakes and stir together. Bring ingredients to a boil, then reduce heat to medium-high. Simmer for 20 minutes until it thickens, stirring frequently.

Ladle the hot berry mixture into warm prepared jars. Use a funnel to safely transfer the mixture, leaving ¼ inch of headspace. Wipe the rims of the jars with a dampened, clean, lint-free cloth or paper towel and again with a dry towel. Place a glass lid with rubber ring in place over the rim of each jar and carefully clip the two metal clamps on each jar directly across from one another. Process in the water bath for 10 minutes. Carefully remove the jars from the water bath with canning tongs and place them on a towel-covered surface for 12 hours without touching. Remove metal clamps and test that the lid has securely sealed onto each jar. Refrigerate after breaking the seal.

RECIPE VARIATION

For a not-so-spicy jam, follow the recipe for spicy blueberry jam but omit the red pepper flakes.

NOTES

BREAD AND BUTTER PICKLES

I adapted this pickle recipe from one I found in my Great-great-grandma Selma's recipe collection. The slices are crisp and crunchy and taste just like a classic bread and butter pickle should. A paring knife or a crinkle cutter tool can be used to slice the cucumbers.

YIELD: **4 WECK** pint jars (8 cups)

3 lb. (9 cups) pickling cucumbers*, sliced into ⅛-inch pieces

3 cups onions, thinly sliced (use a mandolin if possible)

water, as needed

½ cup canning salt

ice, as needed (for soaking pickles in ice bath)

2 cups organic or non-GMO granulated sugar

2 cups organic apple cider vinegar

1 tsp. celery seed

2 tbsp. yellow mustard seeds

Wash each pickling cucumber, gently scrubbing off any dirt. Trim off the ends as well as any flawed or bruised areas, and discard any soft cucumbers. Add cucumber and onion slices to a large nonreactive container such as a stainless-steel pot or glass bowl, and cover with water. Stir in canning salt, cover with ice, and allow to soak for 2 hours; add more ice as needed. This ice/salt bath will keep the pickles crunchy during processing. After 2 hours, drain and rinse with cold water. Strain cucumber and onion slices and set aside.

In a large nonreactive pot, combine the sugar, vinegar, celery seeds, and mustard seeds, heat to a simmer, and stir until the sugar is dissolved. Meanwhile, pack the jars with the cucumber and onion slices. Pack them in the jars as tightly as possible without crushing or bruising them. If you pack them too loosely, you'll end up with a jar full of brine and floating pickle slices.

Ladle the hot brine over the pickles. Use a funnel to safely transfer the mixture, leaving ¼ inch of headspace. Use a butter knife to remove any air bubbles trapped in the jars; add more brine if needed. Wipe the rims of the jars with a dampened, clean, lint-free cloth or paper towel and again with a dry towel. Place a glass lid with rubber ring in place over the rim of each jar and carefully clip the two metal clamps on each jar directly across from one another. Process in the water bath for 10 minutes. Carefully remove the jars from the water bath with canning tongs and place them on a towel-covered surface for 12 hours without touching. Remove metal clamps and test that the lid has securely sealed onto each jar. Allow the flavors to meld for at least two weeks before opening. Refrigerate after breaking the seal.

NOTES

*Small pickling cucumbers (3 to 4 inches long when whole) are ideal for this recipe; they'll stay crunchier after processing. Freshness plays a huge factor in the firmness of pickles so be sure to use fresh cukes that have been harvested within the last 24 to 48 hours.

SPICY BRUSSELS SPROUT PICKLES

These brussels sprout pickles are on my annual must-make list. Everyone who tries them loves them—even the kids!

YIELD: **2 WECK** pint jars (4 cups)

3 cups brussels sprouts*
6 garlic cloves, sliced
2 tsp. yellow mustard seeds
2 tsp. dill seeds
2 tsp. red pepper flakes (add more
   for more spice)

BRINE:

2 cups water
2 cups white distilled vinegar
   (5 percent acidity)
2 tbsp. canning salt

Clean brussels sprouts by soaking them, trimming off the ends, and removing the outer layer of leaves. Cut away any blemishes. In a nonreactive pot, bring the brine ingredients to a boil, stir until the salt is dissolved, then reduce heat to a low simmer.

Divide the garlic, mustards seeds, dill seeds, and red pepper flakes between the jars. Pack the jars with brussels sprouts and fit them in as snugly as possible without damaging them.

Ladle the brine over the filled jars, leaving ¼ inch of headspace. Wipe the rims of the jars with a dampened, clean, lint-free cloth or paper towel and again with a dry towel. Place a glass lid with rubber ring in place over the rim of each jar and carefully clamp the two metal clamps on each jar directly across from one another. Process in the water bath for 10 minutes. Carefully remove the jars from the water bath with canning tongs and place them on a towel-covered surface for 12 hours without touching. Remove metal clamps and test that the lid has securely sealed onto each jar. Refrigerate after breaking the seal.

RECIPE VARIATION

Instead of using hot pepper flakes to add spice, add your favorite spicy pepper. Wash, trim off the ends, slice or cut the pepper in half, and pack into each jar with the brussels sprouts.

NOTES

*Baby brussels sprouts are preferable for this recipe as they are more tender and fit better in the jars. Larger brussels sprouts will work but should be cut in half.

CAULIFLOWER AND BEET PICKLES (REFRIGERATOR RECIPE)

These dark pink pickles brighten up any snack platter and are a welcome pop of color and flavor in salads.

YIELD: I WECK quart jar

3 cups cauliflower florets
I cup beets, chopped and peeled

BRINE:

I cup red wine vinegar (6 percent acidity)
I cup water
I tsp. canning salt
½ tsp. whole peppercorns

Prepare cauliflower and beets. In a small nonreactive saucepan, bring brine ingredients to a simmer. Once the salt has dissolved, add the cauliflower and beets. Bring to a simmer, then set timer and cook 2 minutes. Do not overcook or the vegetables will become soft. Remove from heat and allow to cool. Carefully ladle the warm mixture into a clean quart WECK jar. Once cooled, close jar and refrigerate.

NOTES

CARROT CAKE JAM

This is my adaptation of carrot cake jam without any added liquid or powdered pectin.

YIELD: **3 WECK jam jars (3 cups)**

1 cup (3 whole) carrots, peeled and coined + ½ cup carrots, peeled and grated for later use

1 cup apple, peeled, cored, diced into small chunks

1 cup pineapple chunks

2 cups organic or non-GMO granulated sugar

2 tbsp. lemon juice

½ tsp. ground cinnamon

¼ tsp. ground nutmeg (optional)

½ tsp. vanilla extract

In a small saucepan, steam or boil 1 cup carrots until tender (20 to 30 minutes), then remove from heat. Once cooled, use a hand blender to purée the carrots (add 1 to 2 spoonsful of water if needed). In a large nonreactive pot, add the puréed carrots, grated carrots, and all remaining ingredients; stir well. Bring to a boil and reduce heat to a medium-high simmer. Simmer for 10 minutes or so until the apples are tender; stir often to avoid burning the jam. When the apple chunks can be pierced easily with a fork, they are done. (Hard apples typically take longer to cook while soft apples are quicker; adjust cook time as needed.)

Ladle the hot fruit mixture into warm prepared jars. Use a funnel to safely transfer the mixture, leaving ¼ inch of headspace. Wipe the rims of the jars with a dampened, clean, lint-free cloth or paper towel and again with a dry towel. Place a glass lid with rubber ring in place over the rim of each jar and carefully clip the two metal clamps on each jar directly across from one another. Process in the water bath for 10 minutes. Carefully remove the jars from the water bath with canning tongs and place them on a towel-covered surface for 12 hours without touching. Remove metal clamps and test that the lid has securely sealed onto each jar. Refrigerate after breaking the seal.

Note: Because there is no added pectin in this recipe, the jam may have a slightly more sauce-like consistency. It tends to firm up once refrigerated.

NOTES

CILANTRO-LIME PICKLED PINEAPPLE

This pickled pineapple is a great ingredient to add to a freshly made tomato salsa. The recipe was created by Illene Sofranko, founder of the Urban Canning Company located in St. Petersburg, Florida. She was taught to can by her Uncle Ray and though she continues to practice traditional methods, she strives to create unique flavor combinations within her canned goods.

YIELD: **4 WECK** pint jars (8 cups)

flesh of 1 whole pineapple, cut into chunks

8 sprigs fresh cilantro (stems and all)

4 limes, sliced

2 jalapeño peppers, sliced

BRINE:

4 cups organic apple cider vinegar

¼ cup organic or non-GMO granulated sugar

1 tbsp. pickling salt

Prepare pineapple by washing the fruit in its entirety (soak in 50/50 water-vinegar bath for 10 minutes), then cut away the skin and core of the pineapple and cut the fruit into chunks. Tip: a bread knife works wonders for cutting away the tough skin of the pineapple.

In a large nonreactive heavy bottomed pot, prepare brine: apple cider vinegar, sugar, and salt. Bring to a boil until the salt and sugar have dissolved. Fill jars evenly with cilantro, lime slices, jalapeño slices, and pineapple chunks. Pack the pineapple in the jars well without crushing or damaging the chunks.

Carefully ladle the hot brine over the pineapple. Use a funnel to safely transfer the mixture, leaving ¼ inch of headspace. Wipe the rims of the jars with a dampened, clean, lint-free cloth or paper towel and again with a dry towel. Place a glass lid with rubber ring in place over the rim of each jar and carefully clip the two metal clamps on each jar directly across from one another. Process in the water bath for 15 minutes. Carefully remove the jars from the water bath with canning tongs and place them on a towel-covered surface for 12 hours without touching. Remove metal clamps and test that the lid has securely sealed onto each jar. Refrigerate after breaking the seal.

NOTES

CRANBERRY-APPLE CHUTNEY

This chutney is the perfect accompaniment to any fall or winter dinner! It tastes great with smoked proteins, over brie or goat cheese on crostini, used as a sandwich condiment, or even spread over freshly baked bread.

YIELD: **6 WECK jam jars (6 cups)**

2 cups (2 medium) apples, peeled, cored, and finely diced

6 cups whole fresh cranberries

½ cup red onion, finely chopped

1 cup golden raisins

2 cups organic or non-GMO granulated sugar

1 cup organic or non-GMO brown sugar

¼ cup organic apple cider vinegar

½ cup orange juice

1 tsp. ground cinnamon

1 tsp. ground ginger or 1 tbsp. fresh ginger root, minced

1 tsp. canning salt

Pick through the cranberries and discard any damaged, soft, or unripe (green, white, or pink) berries as well as stems; rinse well. Add all ingredients into a large nonreactive heavy bottomed pot and mix well, stirring until the sugar has dissolved. Bring ingredients to a boil, then reduce heat to medium-high and simmer for about 12 minutes, stirring often.

Ladle the hot fruit mixture into warm prepared jars. Use a funnel to safely transfer the mixture, leaving ¼ inch of headspace. Wipe the rims of the jars with a dampened, clean, lint-free cloth or paper towel and again with a dry towel. Place a glass lid with rubber ring in place over the rim of each jar and carefully clip the two metal clamps on each jar directly across from one another. Process in the water bath for 15 minutes. Carefully remove the jars from the water bath with canning tongs and place them on a towel-covered surface for 12 hours without touching. Remove metal clamps and test that the lid has securely sealed on each jar. Refrigerate after breaking the seal.

RECIPE VARIATION

Consider adding red pepper flakes to add spice or 1 tsp. ground clove for an alternate flavor.

NOTES

CRANBERRY SAUCE

Cranberry sauce is by far one of the easiest canning endeavors. The sauce is full of flavor that cannot compare to any commercially processed sauce. Make a batch of this as a quick side dish over the holidays or gift it to the host of your next family gathering. It's great to have on hand for last minute dinners. There will be no disappointing with this beautiful red, sweet, and tart sauce. When serving, consider stirring in nuts, raisins, or some fresh orange zest.

YIELD: **2–3 WECK pint jars (5–6 cups)**

8 cups (2 lb.) fresh cranberries

2 cups organic or non-GMO granulated sugar

2 cups water

½ tsp. ground allspice (optional)

½ tsp. ground cloves (optional)

Pick through cranberries and discard any damaged, soft, or unripe berries (pink, white or greenish colored). Rinse thoroughly. In a large pot, stir together sugar and water and bring to a boil, stirring until the sugar is completely dissolved. Add cranberries and return to a boil. Reduce heat to a medium-high simmer and cook for 10 minutes, stirring occasionally. As the berries simmer, you will begin to hear them "pop" as they split apart. At this point, add in the optional ingredients of allspice and ground cloves if you so choose and stir well.

Ladle the hot berry mixture into warm prepared jars. Use a funnel to safely transfer the mixture, leaving ¼ inch of headspace. Wipe the rims of the jars with a dampened, clean, lint-free cloth or paper towel and again with a dry towel. Place a glass lid with rubber ring in place over the rim of each jar and carefully clip the two metal clamps on each jar directly across from one another. Process in the water bath for 15 minutes. Carefully remove the jars from the water bath with canning tongs and place them on a towel-covered surface for 12 hours without touching. Remove metal clamps and test that the lid has securely sealed onto each jar. Refrigerate after breaking the seal.

NOTES

DICED TOMATOES

If you've ever successfully grown tomatoes in your garden, you know that there comes a point at the end of the season where you suddenly find yourself with more tomatoes than you know what to do with. If this happens, preserve a few jars!

YIELD: 3–4 WECK pint jars or
2 WECK quart jars (9 cups)

5 lbs. fresh tomatoes (about
   8 cups diced)

3–6 tbsp. lemon juice

½ tsp. canning salt, fresh basil, red
   pepper flakes, oregano, garlic
   powder, thyme, or rosemary
   (optional)

Wash, core and dice tomatoes into uniform-size pieces. Cut away any bruised or flawed areas. In a large heavy-bottomed pot, heat tomatoes to a boil, then reduce heat to a simmer for 5 minutes. Add 1 tbsp. lemon juice to each jar and the optional ingredients, if desired. (If you decide to use quart-size WECK jars for preserving, use 2 tbsp. of lemon juice per jar.)

Ladle the hot tomatoes into warm prepared jars. Use a funnel to safely transfer the mixture, leaving ¼ inch of headspace. Push down the tomatoes so the juice rises over the diced tomatoes. Wipe the rims of the jars with a dampened, clean, lint-free cloth or paper towel and again with a dry towel. Place a glass lid with rubber ring in place over the rim of each jar and carefully clip the two metal clamps on each jar directly across from one another. Process in the water bath for 35 minutes (or 40 minutes if using quart-size jars). Carefully remove the jars from the water bath with canning tongs and place them on a towel-covered surface for 24 hours without touching. Remove metal clamps and test that the lid has securely sealed onto each jar. Refrigerate after breaking the seal.

RECIPE VARIATION

If you prefer whole or halved tomatoes instead of diced, you must first and blanch them. To blanch the tomatoes, submerge them in boiling water until the skin starts to split, about 1 to 2 minutes, then quickly and carefully remove them from the boiling water with a slotted spoon and submerge them into an ice bath. (Reserve the boiled water; you may need it later.) Repeat this process until all tomatoes have been blanched. This method will make it easy to remove the skins with the rub of your fingers. Once the skin has been removed, core the tomatoes.

Add 1 tbsp. lemon juice to each jar if using a 2-cup jar or 2 tbsp. to each jar if using a 3–4 cup jar, as well as optional ingredients. Fill warm prepared jars with tomatoes, leaving ¼ inch of headspace, and push them down without crushing them, until the space between them fills with juice. Use a butter knife to remove any air pockets trapped within the jars and the tomatoes. If the natural tomato juices do not fill the jar enough to reach ¼ inch of headspace, use warm water from the blanching process to fill the jars to ¼ inch of headspace.

Wipe the rims of the jars with a dampened, clean, lint-free cloth or paper towel and again with a dry towel. Place the glass lid with rubber ring in place over the rim of the jar and carefully clip the two metal clamps on the jar directly across from one another. Process in the water bath for 85 minutes. Carefully remove the jars from the water bath with canning tongs and place them on a towel-covered surface for 24 hours without touching. Remove metal clamps and test that the lid has securely sealed onto each jar. Refrigerate after breaking the seal.

GREEN-CHERRY-TOMATO SWEET RELISH

Before each frost of the season, I harvest all the green tomatoes from my plants, leaving me with more than I know what to do with. Over the years I've found creative ways to preserve them. This relish is a great substitute for any sweet pickle relish you'd normally use on sandwiches, burgers, or mixed in salads, deviled eggs, tartar sauce, tuna salad, and so on.

YIELD: **4 WECK** jam jars (4 cups)

3½ cups green tomatoes, halved

1½ cups (1 whole) onion, diced

½ cup (½ of 1 whole) green bell pepper, diced

½ cup (½ of 1 whole) red bell pepper, diced

1½ cups organic or non-GMO granulated sugar

1 cup organic apple cider vinegar or distilled white vinegar (5 percent acidity)

1 tsp. canning salt

1 tsp. yellow mustard seed

1 tsp. celery seed

Use a food processor to finely chop the tomatoes, onion, and peppers. In a large nonreactive heavy-bottomed pot, bring sugar, vinegar, and salt to a boil; stir until the sugar is dissolved. Add the remaining ingredients, mix well, and bring to a boil, then reduce heat to medium-high and simmer for 8 minutes. Stir frequently.

Fill warm prepared jars with the relish, leaving ¼ inch of headspace. Wipe the rims of the jars with a dampened, clean, lint-free cloth or paper towel and again with a dry towel. Place a glass lid with rubber ring in place over the rim of each jar and carefully clip the two metal clamps on each jar directly across from one another. Process in the water bath for 10 minutes. Carefully remove the jars from the water bath with canning tongs and place them on a towel-covered surface for 12 hours without touching. Remove metal clamps and test that the lid has securely sealed onto each jar. Refrigerate after breaking the seal.

NOTES

GROUND HORSERADISH ROOT (REFRIGERATOR RECIPE)

There is no approved method for canning offered by the USDA, but this quick refrigerator recipe will last at least a few weeks. Horseradish is delicious mixed with cocktail sauce and enjoyed with poached, chilled shrimp. It's wonderful mixed with mayo or plain yogurt to make a creamy sauce that can be enjoyed with prime rib or steak. It's also a fantastic spread on a sandwich or wrap or mixed into my Bloody Mary Mix (pg. 47).

YIELD: **3 Mini Mold WECK jars, (¾ cup)**

1 cup horseradish root*, peeled, cubed
¼ tsp. canning salt
½ cup white distilled vinegar
  (5 percent acidity)

Add prepared horseradish root to a food processer and blend. Once chopped, the oils in the root become exposed to the air and will make the ground root spicy. Vinegar will stop this reaction, so if you want a hot horseradish, allow it to sit for 5 to 10 minutes before adding vinegar; if you want a milder flavor, move on to the next step immediately.

Once ready, add remaining ingredients to the food processor and blend together. If the horseradish seems to dry, add in a little more vinegar and blend again. Repeat until the ground horseradish reaches the ideal consistency. Transfer to clean WECK jars, add the orange rubber ring and glass lid to each jar, securely clip on the clamps directly across from one another, and refrigerate. Best if used within 4 weeks.

NOTES

*Warning: the blended horseradish root will take your breath away so be sure to keep a safe distance when removing the blended root from the food processor.

HOT PEPPER AND APPLE JAM

This recipe is my twist on pepper jelly. My brother-in-law has asked me several times to make pepper jelly, but because most recipes call for added pectin (which I don't typically use), I developed this spicy apple jam that is a mighty-fine substitute, as far as I'm concerned. It's very versatile and can be used as you would a chutney, but it's also great over cheese and crackers.

YIELD: **4 WECK jam jars (4 cups)**

4 cups (5 whole) apples, peeled, diced

1 cup hot peppers, diced

½ tsp. canning salt

1½ cups organic or non-GMO granulated sugar

¼ cup honey

¼ cup lemon juice

1 tsp. ground ginger

1 tsp. ground cinnamon

In a large sauce pan, add the apples, hot peppers, salt, sugar, and honey; mix well. Bring to a boil, then reduce heat to a medium-high simmer for 15 minutes, stirring often. Add lemon juice, ground ginger, and ground cinnamon; mix well and simmer an additional 5 minutes.

Ladle the hot fruit mixture into warm prepared jars. Use a funnel to safely transfer the mixture, leaving ¼ inch of headspace. Wipe the rims of the jars with a dampened, clean, lint-free cloth or paper towel and again with a dry towel. Place a glass lid with rubber ring in place over the rim of each jar and carefully clip the two metal clamps on each jar directly across from one another. Process in the water bath for 15 minutes. Carefully remove the jars from the water bath with canning tongs and place them on a towel-covered surface for 12 hours without touching. Remove metal clamps and test that the lid has securely sealed onto each jar. Refrigerate after breaking the seal.

NOTES

PAPAYA CHUTNEY

In the spring of 2017, papayas were on sale at my local co-op. I had never preserved papayas before and decided to experiment with them. Though the other recipes I made were duds, this chutney is out-of-this-world delicious!

YIELD: **4–5 WECK jam jars (4½ cups)**

8 cups (2 whole) papayas, peeled, halved lengthwise, and diced

1 cup red onion, diced

⅔ cup golden raisins

2 tbsp. lime juice

2 tbsp. lemon juice

¼ cup orange juice

¼ cup organic apple cider vinegar

2 tsp fresh ginger, grated or finely chopped

2 cups organic or non-GMO granulated sugar

1 cup brown sugar, organic

1 tsp. red pepper flakes

1 tsp. ground cinnamon

1 tsp. canning salt

Choose papayas without blemishes that are yellow in color. Wash the skin, cut the papaya in half lengthwise, and scoop out the seeds. Peel the papayas with a potato peeler and dice the fruit into chunks. Add all ingredients into a large heavy-bottomed nonreactive pot and mix well. Bring ingredients to a medium-high simmer and cook for 50 to 55 minutes, stirring often. Once the papaya is soft and most of the liquid has cooked away, the chutney is ready to be canned.

Ladle the hot fruit mixture into warm prepared jars. Use a funnel to safely transfer the mixture, leaving ¼ inch of headspace. Wipe the rims of the jars with a dampened, clean, lint-free cloth or paper towel and again with a dry towel. Place a glass lid with rubber ring in place over the rim of each jar and carefully clip the two metal clamps on each jar directly across from one another. Process in the water bath for 15 minutes. Carefully remove the jars from the water bath with canning tongs and place them on a towel-covered surface for 12 hours without touching. Remove metal clamps and test that the lid has securely sealed onto each jar. Refrigerate after breaking the seal.

NOTES

PICKLED GARLIC-DILL ASPARAGUS SPEARS

These salty, garlicky spears make a wonderful replacement for any regular cucumber dill pickle. They are a beautiful addition to a relish platter and a perfect garnish in a Bloody Mary (pg. 47).

YIELD: **2 (1L) Cylindrical WECK jars**

3 lb. (60 spears) fresh asparagus*
8 fresh garlic cloves
2 tsp. dried dill seeds
2 tsp. yellow mustard seeds
2. tbsp. red pepper flakes (optional for spice)

BRINE:

3 cups distilled white vinegar (5 percent acidity)
3 cups water
¼ cup pickling salt

Clean the asparagus thoroughly, trim off the ends to fit the canning jar size you are using and remember to leave ¼ inch of headspace. In a nonreactive pot, bring the brine ingredients to a boil and simmer for 3 minutes. Divide the garlic, dill seeds, mustard seeds, and optional red pepper flakes between the warm prepared canning jars. Pack the jars with asparagus as tightly as possible without bruising or damaging the spears.

Ladle the hot brine over the spears, leaving ¼ inch of headspace. Wipe the rims of the jars with a dampened, clean, lint-free cloth or paper towel and again with a dry towel. Place a glass lid with rubber ring in place over the rim of each jar and carefully clip the two metal clamps on each jar directly across from one another. Process in the water bath for 10 minutes. Carefully remove the jars from the water bath with canning tongs and place them on a towel-covered surface for 12 hours without touching. Remove metal clamps and test that the lid has securely sealed onto each jar. Allow the flavors to meld at least two weeks before opening. Refrigerate after breaking the seal.

*Medium-sized asparagus spears are ideal for this recipe. Too-thin spears risk becoming too tender (soft) and too-thick spears take up too much room in the jars.

NOTES

PICKLED GREEN TOMATOES (REFRIGERATOR RECIPE)

My grandpa made these pickles when I was a kid and I loved them; the spicier the better. Green cherry tomatoes or larger variety unripened tomatoes can be used interchangeably.

YIELD: **2 WECK pint jars (4 cups)**

4 cups green tomatoes, halved or cut into chunks for larger tomatoes

4 cloves garlic, halved

2 jalapeño peppers, halved (for more spice add more peppers or a spicier variety)

BRINE:

1 cup water

1 cup white distilled vinegar (5 percent acidity)

1 tsp. canning salt

Wash tomatoes, removing any flawed areas and stems. Heat the brine ingredients to a simmer and stir until salt is dissolved. Reduce heat and allow to cool. Divide tomatoes, garlic, and peppers between two warm prepared WECK pint jars.

Ladle the warm brine over the tomatoes, leaving ¼ inch of headspace. Use a stainless-steel butter knife or other tool to get rid of any air bubbles trapped within the peppers and jars. Wipe the rims of the jars with a dampened, clean, lint-free cloth or paper towel and again with a dry towel. Place a glass lid with rubber ring in place over the rim of each jar and carefully clip the two metal clamps on each jar directly across from one another. Allow the jars to cool, then store them in the refrigerator. Though the pickles are technically edible immediately, I recommend letting the flavors meld for at least 2 weeks before enjoying. The longer they pickle, the tastier they get.

NOTES

PICKLED MUSHROOMS

These mushrooms are so delicious! They are fantastic added to an antipasto salad or platter with marinated olives, assorted salamis, and provolone cheese.

YIELD: **2 WECK** pint jars (4 cups)

16 oz. white button mushrooms
5 cloves garlic, chopped
½ small white onion, finely chopped
½ tsp. whole black peppercorns
1 tsp. red pepper flakes per jar (optional)

BRINE:

2 cups distilled white vinegar
  (5 percent acidity)
1 cup water
2 tsp. canning salt

Clean mushrooms, making sure to remove all dirt and flawed/bruised areas. Trim off the ends of the mushroom stems and slice them ⅛–¼ inches thick. In a nonreactive saucepan, bring the brine ingredients to a boil and stir until salt is dissolved. Divide the mushrooms, onion, garlic, optional red pepper flakes, and optional peppercorns between the jars. It is essential to be very mindful when packing the mushroom slices into the jar; if the jars are packed too loosely you will end up with half a jar of just brine. Pack the slices in as firmly as possible without breaking them.

Once the jars are well packed, ladle the hot brine over the mushroom slices. Use a funnel to safely transfer the brine into each jar, leaving ¼ inch of headspace. Use a stainless-steel butter knife or other clean tool to remove any air bubbles trapped within the mushrooms and the jars. Wipe the rims of the jars with a dampened, clean, lint-free cloth or paper towel and again with a dry towel. Place a glass lid with rubber ring in place over the rim of each jar and carefully clip the two metal clamps on each jar directly across from one another. Process in the water bath for 15 minutes. Carefully remove the jars from the water bath with canning tongs and place them on a towel-covered surface for 12 hours without touching. Remove metal clamps and test that the lid has securely sealed onto each jar. Though the peppers are edible immediately, I recommend letting the flavors commingle for a few days before enjoying. Refrigerate after breaking the seal.

NOTES

PICKLED PEPPER SLICES

Pickled peppers are a delicious way to use up the excess pepper harvest before winter. They add a spicy kick to any meal!

YIELD: **2 WECK** pint jars (4 cups)

I lb. hot peppers, mixed variety
4 garlic cloves, halved

BRINE:

1½ cups distilled white vinegar
  (5 percent acidity)
1½ tbsp. canning salt
1½ cups water

Wash peppers, remove stems, slice them ⅛–¼ inches thick, and add them to a large bowl. Once all peppers are sliced, mix well. In a nonreactive pot, bring the brine ingredients to a boil and simmer for 3 minutes. Divide the garlic between the warm prepared canning jars, then pack the jars with hot pepper slices well. Push the pepper slices down carefully without damaging them, otherwise you'll end up with a jar full of brine and only half full of peppers.

Ladle the hot brine over the peppers, leaving ¼ inch of headspace. Use a stainless-steel butter knife or other clean tool to remove any air bubbles trapped within the peppers and the jars. Wipe the rims of the jars with a dampened, clean, lint-free cloth or paper towel and again with a dry towel. Place a glass lid with rubber ring in place over the rim of each jar and carefully clip the two metal clamps on each jar directly across from one another.

Process in the water bath for 10 minutes. Carefully remove the jars from the water bath with canning tongs and place them on a towel-covered surface for 12 hours without touching. Remove metal clamps and test that the lid has securely sealed onto each jar. Though the peppers are edible immediately, I recommend letting the flavors blend for a week or two before enjoying. Refrigerate after breaking the seal.

RECIPE VARIATION

Water-bath sealing the peppers will cause them to lose their crispness. If you want the crunch of the peppers to remain, follow all the directions in the first two paragraphs. Fill the jars with peppers, add the brine, wipe the rims, add the rings, lids, and clamp shut, but do not water-bath seal the jars. Put the sealed jars on a towel-covered surface and let them cool. Once cooled, they need to be refrigerated. The peppers will not be shelf-stable, but they will be flavorful and crisp and last for several months refrigerated.

NOTES

PINEAPPLE-STRAWBERRY JAM

This recipe has been adapted from a recipe I found in my great, great grandma Selma's collection. I refer to it as "spring in a jar."

YIELD: **3 WECK jam jars (3–4 cups)**

3 cups strawberries, quartered

1½ cups fresh pineapple, grated

2½ cups organic or non-GMO
    granulated sugar

Clean and prepare strawberries by cutting off the stems and any flawed/bruised areas. Use a potato masher to mash the quartered berries into a chunky consistency. Combine all ingredients in a large heavy-bottomed pot and mix well. Bring ingredients to a medium-high simmer and cook for 20 to 25 minutes, stirring often. Once mixture has thickened and most of the liquid has cooked away, the jam is ready to be canned.

Ladle the hot fruit mixture into warm prepared jars. Use a funnel to safely transfer the mixture, leaving ¼ inch of headspace. Wipe the rims of the jars with a dampened, clean, lint-free cloth or paper towel and again with a dry towel. Place a glass lid with rubber ring in place over the rim of the jar and carefully clip the two metal clamps on the jar directly across from one another. Process in the water bath for 10 minutes. Carefully remove the jars from the water bath with canning tongs and place them on a towel-covered surface for 12 hours without touching. Remove metal clamps and test that the lid has securely sealed onto the jar. Refrigerate after breaking the seal.

NOTES

POLISH STRAWBERRY KOMPOT (REFRIGERATOR RECIPE)

This recipe has been submitted by Emily and Kryz, the owners of Stone Creek Trading. It's been adapted from a traditional Polish recipe that's been passed down from Kryz's mother. This kompot is a family-favorite and a fantastic way to enjoy excess strawberry harvest during the cold winter months. Emily says, "Traditionally, families make several batches of kompot with varying amounts of sugar for different purposes. If less sugar is used, the thinner the juice will be, which is usually enjoyed over ice in the fall months. If more sugar is used in the recipe, it will result in a sweeter kompot with a thicker syrup, which can be added to hot water to make tea or served over desserts!"

YIELD: **2 WECK quart jars (8 cups)**

1 lb. fresh strawberries

½ cup organic or non-GMO granulated sugar

6 cups water

Wash and prepare strawberries by removing stems and trimming off any bruised areas/blemishes. In a large pot, combine sugar and water and bring to a boil. Once the sugar has dissolved, remove from heat and allow the syrup to cool 5 to 10 minutes.

Pack the WECK jars with berries, filling them ⅔ full. Pour the syrup over the strawberries, leaving ¼ inch of headspace. Let the jars cool fully, then refrigerate. Allow the flavors to unite at least 2 days before enjoying. Use within two weeks. To serve, pour the berry juice into a glass, either diluting with warm or cold water as desired. Add a couple of fresh berries to each glass and enjoy.

NOTES

NOTES

RASPBERRY JAM

This recipe is a classic raspberry jam that was found in my great, great grandmother's recipe collection. It's simple, quick, and comforting to think that this is the same jam my grandmother and many of yours made and enjoyed nearly one hundred years ago.

YIELD: **4 WECK jam jars (4 cups)**

4 cups fresh raspberries
3½ cups organic or non-GMO granulated sugar

Clean and rinse berries, discarding any that are soft or damaged. Add the raspberries to a large pot and use a potato masher to break them down into a sauce-like consistency, then add the sugar. Bring mixture to a boil and reduce heat to simmer. Stir constantly and simmer for only 3 to 5 minutes. If the jam is cooked too long, it will have too stiff of a consistency and will not spread.

Ladle the hot berry mixture into warm prepared jars. Use a funnel to safely transfer the mixture, leaving ¼ inch of headspace. Wipe the rims of the jars with a dampened, clean, lint-free cloth or paper towel and again with a dry towel. Place a glass lid with rubber ring in place over the rim of each jar and carefully clip the two metal clamps on each jar directly across from one another. Process in the water bath for 10 minutes. Carefully remove the jars from the water bath with canning tongs and place them on a towel-covered surface for 12 hours without touching. Remove metal clamps and test that the lid has securely sealed onto each jar. Refrigerate after breaking the seal.

RECIPE VARIATION

We are fortunate to have an abundance of raspberries in the summer, harvested right from our front yard. When preserving them, we always make a batch of raspberry sauce to enjoy over pancakes, waffles, or to bake with. But we especially love mixing the sauce into our homemade ice cream.

To make sauce instead of jam, follow the raspberry jam recipe above but only add 2 cups of sugar, and instead of simmering the mixture for 3 to 5 minutes, simmer only 1 to 2 minutes. This will result in a delicious, pourable sauce. Process in water bath as a jam recipe or allow to cool and refrigerate. If refrigerating, use within 2 weeks.

WHOLE RASPBERRIES IN LIGHT SYRUP

I love to preserve a fruit at the height of its seasonal peak and enjoy it again during the colder months. Preserved whole berries are delicious added to yogurt, pancakes, waffles, smoothies, ice cream, or oatmeal.

YIELD: **3 WECK jam jars (3 cups)**

3½ cups fresh raspberries

LIGHT SYRUP:

½ cup organic or non-GMO granulated sugar
I cup water

Clean and rinse berries, discarding any that are soft or damaged. In a small saucepan, heat water and sugar over medium-high heat and stir until the sugar is dissolved. Pack raspberries into the warm prepared jars.

Ladle the syrup over the raspberries, leaving ¼ inch of headspace. Use a stainless-steel butter knife or other tool to remove any air bubbles trapped within the berries and the jars. Wipe the rims of the jars with a dampened, clean, lint-free cloth or paper towel and again with a dry towel. Place a glass lid with rubber ring in place over the rim of each jar and carefully clip the two metal clamps on each jar directly across from one another. Process in the water bath for 10 minutes. Carefully remove the jars from the water bath with canning tongs and place them on a towel-covered surface for 12 hours without touching. Remove metal clamps and test that the lid has securely sealed onto each jar. Refrigerate after breaking the seal.

RECIPE VARIATION

Instead of using sugar for the syrup, substitute ½ cup honey.

NOTES

RHUBARB SYRUP

Between my mom, grandma, aunt, and myself, we have an endless amount of rhubarb growing in our gardens (all plants originated in two of my great grandmother's gardens and have been passed down for generations). We clean and freeze several cups for winter enjoyment, use much in the summer for pies and other baked treats, and I turn a lot into jam. Aside from strawberry rhubarb jam, my favorite way to preserve rhubarb is by turning it into rhubarb syrup. It is not only a beautiful pink color but is also incredibly delicious, especially served with champagne (think mimosa, but substitute this syrup for orange juice).

YIELD: I WECK quart jar (5 cups)

- 11 cups (11 large stalks or 22 small stalks) rhubarb
- 2 cups water
- 2 cups organic or non-GMO granulated sugar

Clean and prepare the rhubarb by scrubbing away any dirt, trimming off the ends and any flawed areas, and chopping it into ½-inch pieces. Add all ingredients into a large heavy-bottomed pot, mix well, and bring to a medium simmer. Simmer the mixture for 20 to 30 minutes, stirring often, until the rhubarb has broken down. To strain the rhubarb solids from the syrup, I recommend using a large heat-tolerant measuring cup (4 cup or 8 cup) and a fine mesh strainer. Slowly ladle the rhubarb mixture into the strainer and separate the syrup. Stirring the stewed rhubarb in the strainer helps speed up the process. As it gets down to the final drippings, use the back of the spoon to push out the liquid. Discard the rhubarb solids or save them to bake with. Repeat the straining process until all of the rhubarb solids and syrup have been separated. For an even clearer syrup (without solids that tend to sneak through), place a piece or two of cheesecloth in the fine mesh strainer before straining, or run syrup through the fine mesh strainer twice.

Once the syrup is separated, heat it in a medium sauce pan and bring to a boil, then remove from heat and begin ladling the hot syrup into warm prepared jars. Use a funnel to safely transfer the syrup, leaving ¼ inch of headspace. Wipe the rims of the jars with a dampened, clean, lint-free cloth or paper towel and again with a dry towel. Place a glass lid with rubber ring in place over the rim of each jar and carefully clip the two metal clamps on each jar directly across from one another. Process in the water bath for 15 minutes. Carefully remove the jars from the water bath with canning tongs and place them on a towel-covered surface for 12 hours without touching. Remove metal clamps and test that the lid has securely sealed onto each jar. Refrigerate after breaking the seal.

NOTES

SPICY PEAR CHUTNEY

This chutney is a fabulous addition to a cheese and cracker spread, paired with proteins, spooned over Indian-style curries, or used as a glaze on baked proteins or squash.

YIELD: **4 WECK** jam jars (4 cups)

4 pears, peeled and cubed

¼ cup red onions, finely diced

2 garlic cloves, chopped

2 jalapeños or other hot peppers, finely chopped

¼ cup golden raisins

¾ cup brown sugar

1 cup organic apple cider vinegar

1 tsp. canning salt

Add all prepared ingredients to a large nonreactive pot; mix well. Bring to a boil and reduce heat to a medium-high simmer for 20 to 25 minutes until pears have softened, stirring often to avoid burning.

Ladle the hot fruit mixture into warm prepared jars. Use a funnel to safely transfer the mixture, leaving ¼ inch of headspace. Wipe the rims of the jars with a dampened, clean, lint-free cloth or paper towel and again with a dry towel. Place a glass lid with rubber ring in place over the rim of each jar and carefully clip the two metal clamps on each jar directly across from one another. Process in the water bath for 15 minutes. Carefully remove the jars from the water bath with canning tongs and place them on a towel-covered surface for 12 hours without touching. Remove metal clamps and test that the lid has securely sealed onto each jar. Refrigerate after breaking the seal.

NOTES

STRAWBERRY-RHUBARB JAM

This classic flavor combo is my favorite of all time. The sweetness of the strawberries paired with the sourness of the rhubarb is a match made in heaven.

YIELD: **6 WECK** jam jars (6 cups)

5 cups (1½ lb.) strawberries, stems removed, quartered

4 cups (6–8 stalks) rhubarb, chopped into ½-inch slices

¼ cup lemon juice

1 cup water

3 cups organic or non-GMO granulated sugar

Wash fruit well. Use a potato masher to break down the quartered berries to a chunky consistency. Put all ingredients in a large nonreactive heavy-bottomed pot and mix well. Bring mixture to a boil, then reduce to a medium-high heat. Simmer 15 to 20 minutes and stir often to avoid burning. Watch out for flyaway jam splatter—it hurts! If you have a candy thermometer, the temperature you want to reach is 220°F (104°C). Once the sauce mixture has thickened, turn the heat down to low.

Ladle the hot strawberry-rhubarb mixture into warm prepared jars. Use a funnel to safely transfer the mixture, leaving ¼ inch of headspace. Wipe the rims of the jars with a dampened, clean, lint-free cloth or paper towel and again with a dry towel. Place a glass lid with rubber ring in place over the rim of each jar and carefully clip the two metal clamps on each jar directly across from one another. Process in the water bath for 10 minutes. Carefully remove the jars from the water bath with canning tongs and place them on a towel-covered surface for 12 hours without touching. Remove metal clamps and test that the lid has securely sealed onto the jar. Refrigerate after breaking the seal.

RECIPE VARIATION

You can use 2 cups of honey in place of sugar in this recipe, but it will result in a looser jam consistency.

NOTES

FERMENTED RECIPES

BLUEBERRY KVASS

This drink tastes pretty much the way you'd expect it to. It turns bluish in color and has a pleasant blueberry taste. Even the children enjoy this kvass!

YIELD: I WECK 743 Mold Jar (3 cups)

I cup blueberries
2–3 cups water, as needed
I tbsp. raw local honey

Wash blueberries and discard any stems or damaged berries. Add blueberries to a clean jar and give them a gentle smoosh with a spoon to break the skins a bit. Add water to the jar, leaving I inch of headspace. Mix in honey; it will effortlessly dissolve on its own in time. Place the glass lid with rubber ring in place over the rim of the jar and carefully clip the two metal clamps on the jar directly across from one another. Store at room temperature, ideally between 60 to 75°F (15 to 23°C), and keep out of direct sunlight.

Check on the ferment at least twice a day to "burp" it and release any carbon dioxide that has built up during fermentation. Stir the mixture and clip the lid back on. Ferment for 4 to 7 days. Taste a spoonful to determine completion; if it doesn't have much a of blueberry flavor after 4 days, let it keep fermenting. Over-fermenting will result in an alcoholic taste. Strain out berries, reserve the kvass, and store in the refrigerator in an airtight container or jar. Drink within a couple of weeks for best flavor.

Tip: don't toss the strained-out fruit from your kvass! Once the kvass is finished, the fruit is great added to a smoothie or eaten as-is.

NOTES

APPLE-CINNAMON KVASS

YIELD: 1 WECK 743 Mold Jar (3 cups)

1 organic apple, sliced into chunks
1 whole organic cinnamon stick
1 pinch salt (optional)
2–3 cups water, as needed
1 tbsp. raw local honey

Wash the apple and slice, removing the core. Add the apple, cinnamon, and optional salt to a clean jar. Add water to the jar, leaving 1 inch of headspace. Mix in honey; it will effortlessly dissolve on its own in time. Place the glass lid with rubber ring in place over the rim of the jar and carefully clip the two metal clamps on the jar directly across from one another. Store at room temperature, ideally between 60 to 75°F (15 to 23°C), and keep out of direct sunlight.

Check on the ferment at least twice a day to "burp" it and release any carbon dioxide that has built up during fermentation. Stir the mixture and clip the lid back on. Ferment for 4 to 7 days. Taste a spoonful to determine completion; if it doesn't have much a of a cinnamon-apple flavor after 4 days, allow it to keep fermenting. Over-fermenting will result in an alcoholic taste. Strain out fruit, reserve the kvass, and store in the refrigerator in an airtight container or jar. Drink within a couple of weeks for best flavor.

NOTES

PINEAPPLE KVASS

This kvass has a mild pineapple flavor and gets a bit carbonated.

YIELD: 1 WECK 743 Mold Jar (3 cups)

1 cup pineapple chunks
2–3 cups water, as needed
1 tbsp. raw local honey

Add chunks of pineapple to a clean jar, add water to the jar, leaving 1 inch of headspace, and mix in honey; it will effortlessly dissolve on its own in time. Place the glass lid with rubber ring in place over the rim of the jar and carefully clip the two metal clamps on the jar directly across from one another. Store at room temperature, ideally between 60 to 75°F (15 to 23°C), and keep out of direct sunlight.

Check on the ferment at least twice a day to "burp" it and release any carbon dioxide that has built up during fermentation. Stir the mixture and clip the lid back on. Ferment for 4 to 5 days. Taste a spoonful to determine completion; if it doesn't have much a of pineapple flavor after 4 days, let it keep fermenting. Over-fermenting will result in an alcoholic taste. Strain out pineapple, reserve the kvass, and store in the refrigerator in an airtight container or jar. Drink within a couple of weeks for best flavor.

NOTES

POMEGRANATE KVASS

YIELD: 1 WECK 743 Mold Jar (3 cups)

1 cup pomegranate seeds
2–3 cups water, as needed
1 tbsp. raw local honey

Add pomegranate seeds to a clean jar, add water to the jar, leaving 1 inch of headspace, and mix in honey; it will effortlessly dissolve on its own in time. Place the glass lid with rubber ring in place over the rim of the jar and carefully clip the two metal clamps on the jar directly across from one another. Store at room temperature, ideally between 60 to 75°F (15 to 23°C), and keep out of direct sunlight.

Check on the ferment at least twice a day to "burp" it and release any carbon dioxide that has built up during fermentation. Stir the mixture and clip the lid back on. Ferment for 3 to 5 days. Taste a spoonful to determine completion; if it doesn't have much a of pomegranate flavor after 3 days, let it keep fermenting. Over-fermenting will result in an alcoholic taste. Strain out fruit, reserve the kvass, and store in the refrigerator in an airtight container or jar. Drink within a couple of weeks for best flavor.

NOTES

CHERRY SALSA

This salsa is a lovely sweet and spicy springtime addition, fitting for a variety of occasions. It's a great accompaniment to chips or tacos but is also incredible on eggs and over grilled chicken or fish.

YIELD: 1 WECK quart jar (4 cups)

3 cups cherries, deseeded, chopped
1 jalapeño, chopped
1 cup cilantro, chopped
1½ tsp fresh lime juice
⅓ cup red onion, finely chopped
1 tbsp. kosher salt

Mix the prepared ingredients together and pack into a clean WECK jar and add salt. Use a glass lid from a smaller WECK jar to act as a weight to hold down the ingredients under the brine. Place the glass lid with rubber ring in place over the rim of the jar and carefully clip the two metal clamps on the jar directly across from one another. Store at room temperature, ideally between 60 and 75°F (15 and 23°C), and keep out of direct sunlight.

This salsa is delicious immediately but grows in flavor as it ferments. Fermentation duration is between 12 to 48 hours. Taste test this recipe after 12 hours and determine if it's fermented to your liking, or if you'd like to ferment another 36 hours. Once fermentation is complete, refrigerate in an airtight container or jar. This ferment will last up to 2 weeks refrigerated.

NOTES

CURTIDO

Curtido is an El Salvadoran cabbage salad and it can be eaten any way that you'd normally enjoy sauerkraut, but it's also phenomenal added to tacos. I keep finding new ways to incorporate this colorful and delicious ferment with my everyday meals.

YIELD: I WECK quart jar (4 cups)

1 head organic cabbage
2 carrots, grated
1 onion, thinly sliced
2 jalapeños, thinly sliced
1½ tbsp. kosher salt
4 garlic cloves, finely chopped
1 tsp. dried or 1 tbsp. fresh oregano
1 tsp. fresh lime juice

In a large glass bowl, mix together the cabbage, carrots, onion, and jalapeños and massage with salt. Once the natural liquid begins to release from the veggies, pack the mixture and all remaining ingredients into a large WECK jar, leaving 1 to 2 inches of headspace. Within an hour, there should be enough liquid (brine) to cover the cabbage mixture completely. If there is not enough brine to cover the cabbage, mix extra brine by dissolving 1 tbsp. salt with 2 cups water. Add brine to the jar until the cabbage shreds are completely covered. Use a glass lid or two from a smaller WECK jar as a weight to hold the vegetables underneath the brine. Add the WECK jar glass lid and ring and clamp it shut or cover jar with cheesecloth or other breathable cover to keep dust and bugs from entering your ferment. If you choose to clip the lid on versus using cheesecloth to cover your ferment, you must "burp" this ferment 1 to 2 times a day to allow any built-up carbon dioxide to release. Store at room temperature, ideally between 60 to 75°F (15 to 23°C), and keep out of direct sunlight.

This is a 7- to 10-day ferment. Be sure to check on the ferment every few days to make sure the brine remains over the cabbage and that no mold has begun to grow. It is completely normal to see little bubbles or even foam-like bubbling occur at the top of the ferment. If the brine is low, use a clean finger or utensil to press down the weight to bring the brine back over the ferment. Taste test after 7 days to determine if the flavor is ideal or if you'd like to ferment a few more days. Once fermentation is complete, store in glass airtight jars and refrigerate.

NOTES

ESCABECHE

This is my adaptation of spicy pickled vegetables that are more commonly pickled in vinegar. These fermented veggies become spicy and delicious. They can be served on the side of meals or used as condiment.

YIELD: 1 WECK quart jar (4 cups)

1 cup cauliflower florets, cut into bite-size uniform pieces
½ cup (skin on) carrots, cut into ¼-inch slices
½ cup red onion, sliced
2 cups hot peppers, thinly sliced
4 garlic cloves, halved
½ tsp. peppercorns (optional)
bay leaf, fresh oregano, or cloves (optional)
1 grape leaf or other leaf with tannins (optional, to keep the veggies crunchy)

BRINE:

1 tbsp. kosher salt dissolved in 2 cups water

Pack jar with prepared ingredients, adding the garlic and optional peppercorns at the bottom. Tuck the optional bay leaf on the side without breaking it. Pour the brine over the veggie mix until they are completely submerged, leaving 1½ inches of headspace. Use a smaller WECK jar lid or two as a weight to hold the veggies underneath the brine. Add the WECK jar glass ring and lid and clamp the jar shut.

Ferment at room temperature, ideally between 60 to 75°F (15 to 23°C), and keep out of direct sunlight. Check on the ferment every day to make sure the brine remains over the produce, and "burp" the ferment daily to allow any built-up carbon dioxide to release. If the brine is low, press down the weight to bring the brine back over the ferment. This is a 7-day ferment. Once fermentation is complete, store in an airtight container or jar and refrigerate.

NOTES

FIERY CIDER

Chances are you've heard of "fire cider" before, originally coined by herbalist Rosemary Gladstar in the 1980s. It's a fermented drink commonly known as a health tonic that kicks the butt of illnesses! It's known to shorten the duration of the common cold, help inflammation, and even reduce high blood pressure. Each ingredient offers a plethora of goodness, and once all is infused together, it's the ultimate immune defense. There is no wrong way to make this recipe, so feel free to play around with ingredients and tweak it to your liking. I generally add ½ cup of each ingredient except for turmeric (¼ cup). All ingredients should be organic.

YIELD: I WECK quart jar (3½ cups)

½ cup fresh ginger root, peeled, cut into ¼-inch slices

½ cup fresh horseradish root, peeled, cut into ¼-inch cubes

¼ cup fresh turmeric root, cut into ¼-inch slices

½ cup onion

10 garlic cloves, crushed

½ cup jalapeños or other hot peppers

1 fresh lemon, sliced and seeds removed or juice and zest from 1 lemon

1 tbsp. raw local honey (optional)

organic apple cider vinegar, as needed

Add ginger, horseradish, turmeric, onion, garlic, jalapeños or other hot peppers, fresh lemon slices or juice and zest, and optional honey to a WECK jar. Fill with apple cider vinegar, leaving 1 inch of headspace. Use lid from smaller glass WECK jar to push the ingredients under the apple cider vinegar. Place the orange rubber ring and glass lid on jar and clamp it shut. Infuse at room temperature and out of direct sunlight at least 4 weeks. There is no need to lift the lid and "burp" this infusion, though you could tip the jar upside down occasionally to mix up the ingredients. Store this fiery cider in an airtight container or jar and refrigerate.

To serve, strain out the solids and enjoy the cider chilled, straight up, over ice, or mixed with water or juice to cut the potency. I prefer to mix about 2 ounces with a little orange juice and have found that the flavor is one that tends to grow on you the more you try it. Get creative with ways in which to use the leftover solids; I add them to a batch of homemade broth and allow them to simmer for 24 hours.

RECIPE VARIATION

Add orange juice, orange zest, or fresh herbs to create new tonic flavors during the infusion process. The combinations are endless!

NOTES

PICKLED GARLIC CLOVES

Whole fermented cloves can be eaten as an immune booster when you're beginning to feel under the weather, or they can be used in homemade salad dressings or marinades.

YIELD: 1 WECK jam jar (1 cup)

¾ cup (1–2 bulbs) organic garlic

BRINE:

1 tsp. kosher salt dissolved in 1 cup water

Peel garlic and cut away any flawed areas. Add it to a clean jar and pour the brine over the cloves. Use a lid from a smaller WECK jar as a weight to hold the garlic under the brine. Place the orange rubber ring and glass lid on the jar and clamp it shut. Ferment at room temperature, ideally between 60 to 75°F (15 to 23°C), and keep out of direct sunlight.

This is a 7-day ferment. Be sure to check on the ferment every day to "burp" it and allow any built-up carbon dioxide to release. Make sure the brine remains over the garlic. If the brine is low, press down the weight to bring the brine back over the ferment. Taste test after 7 days to determine if the flavor is ideal or if you'd like to ferment a few days, weeks, or months more. Once fermentation is complete, store in an airtight container or jar and refrigerate.

NOTES

GIARDINIERA

This recipe is one of my absolute favorite ferments. It's a welcomed condiment for sandwiches, eggs, pizza, pasta, salads, and pretty much everything. Really, try it!

YIELD: I WECK quart jar (4 cups)

½ cup (1–2 whole) carrots, unpeeled, chopped

I cup (2–3 stalks) celery, sliced into ¼-inch pieces

2 cloves garlic, chopped

I cup (5–6 whole peppers) serrano peppers, sliced ¼-inch-thick

I cup cauliflower florets

I grape leaf or other leaf with tannins (optional, to keep the ingredients crunchy)

BRINE:

I tbsp. kosher salt dissolved in 2 cups water

Mix all vegetables together and transfer to the WECK jar. The natural tannins from a grape leaf, raspberry leaf, oak leaf, or other leaf with tannins will help keep the vegetables crunchy but is not required. Pour brine over the vegetables, completely covering the mixture by ½ to 1 inch and use the lid from a smaller WECK jar or two, if more weight is needed to hold the veggies under the brine. Leave 1 to 2 inches of headspace for the veggies to ferment and bubble. This is a very active ferment, so expect a lot of bubbles. Add the WECK jar ring and glass lid and clamp it shut or cover jar with cheesecloth or other breathable cover to keep dust and bugs from entering your ferment. If you choose to clip the lid on versus using cheesecloth to cover your ferment, you must "burp" this ferment 2 times a day to allow any built-up carbon dioxide to release. Store at room temperature, ideally between 60 to 75°F (15 to 23°C), and keep out of direct sunlight.

This is a 7-day ferment. Be sure to check on the ferment every day to make sure the brine remains over the mix and that no mold or yeast has begun to grow. If the brine is low, use a clean finger or utensil to press down the weight(s) to bring the brine back over the ferment. Once fermentation is complete, store in an airtight container or jar and refrigerate.

NOTES

GINGERY BEET KVASS

Not enough good can be said about beets! They are rich in antioxidants, known to lower cholesterol levels, and act as a natural detoxifier. Kvass in general is known to help the digestive system so this probiotic drink can't be beet (get it?)!

YIELD: 1 WECK quart jar (4 cups)

3-4 small (skin on) beets, cut into 1–2-
   inch pieces
2-inch chunk fresh ginger root (or more
   for more potency), coined
water, as needed
1 tsp. kosher salt

Wash beets, trim off ends and greens, and cut into uniform-size pieces. Fill jar with beets and ginger and add water, leaving 1 to 2 inches of headspace. Stir in salt and mix well. Cover the WECK jar with the rubber ring and glass lid, and clamp it shut. Ferment at room temperature, ideally between 60 to 75°F (15 to 23°C), and keep out of direct sunlight.

Open the lid once a day to "burp" the ferment, releasing any built-up carbon dioxide. This is a 4- to 6-day ferment; taste to determine completion. Once fermentation is complete, strain out beets and ginger, reserve the kvass in a clean jar, add rubber ring and lid, clamp shut, and refrigerate. Best if enjoyed within 3 weeks.

NOTES

WHAT'S KIMCHI GOOD WITH?

I'm the wrong person to ask because I think kimchi goes with just about everything. I'm a bit of a "kimchi addict," if you will. My love for kimchi is what got me started fermenting in the first place. I love to devour a bowl of it straight from the jar, though it's a phenomenal addition to scrambled eggs. I really enjoy adding it to my homemade bone broth with a couple of poached eggs to make a healthy and flavor-packed soup. I have added it to grilled cheese sandwiches, mixed it with macaroni and cheese, and even topped homemade pizza with it (surprisingly delicious!). Oh, and it's fantastic to make cauliflower fried "rice" with, though I typically enjoy my ferments uncooked or gently cooked to get the most benefit from them; heating ferments kills off the good bacteria that is created during fermentation.

KIMCHI (VEGAN-FRIENDLY)

YIELD: **2 WECK** quart jars (8 cups)

2 heads napa cabbage
¼ cup kosher salt
daikon radishes (optional)
carrots (optional)

KIMCHI PEPPER PASTE:

6 cloves garlic
2-inch piece ginger root or more if desired, peeled
1 medium onion
¾ cup gochugaru (coarse hot pepper powder)
1 tbsp. cayenne pepper (optional)
1-2 tbsp. Red Boat Fish Sauce or other preservative-free fish sauce*
(optional)
5 green onions, cut into 1-inch pieces

Remove the outer leaves of the cabbage and wash the cabbage well between each leaf. Cut each head of cabbage in half lengthwise and rinse again with cold water. Remove the core of each cabbage and cut the cabbages into 1- to 2-inch bite-size pieces. In a large nonreactive container such as a stainless-steel pot or glass bowl, add the cabbage, salt, and optional ingredients and mix together well while gently massaging the cabbage and salt together with your hands. The salt not only gives the cabbage flavor, but also tenderizes it. Once the cabbage is evenly salted, allow the cabbage to sit for 4 hours. As the salted cabbage shrinks, the natural brine is created. Stir once halfway through the salting process.

For the kimchi pepper paste, use a food processor to purée the garlic, ginger, and onion. In a separate bowl, mix this purée together with the gochugaru (coarse pepper powder), optional cayenne, and optional preservative-free fish sauce to create a paste. Fish sauce adds a surprisingly delicious flavor complexity to the kimchi, though it's still outstanding without it. Clean the green onions by removing their root ends and the thin outer layer and add 1-inch pieces to the hot pepper paste.

*Note: non-vegan ingredient.

Continued on next page

Once the cabbage has reached the saltiness desired (after 4 hours or so), add the kimchi paste to the salted cabbage and mix well. Transfer kimchi as well as all the natural brine into clean WECK jars, pushing down cabbage to pack it into each jar, leaving 2 inches of headspace so the jars do not overflow during fermentation. Add the orange rubber WECK jar ring and lid to each jar, and clip jars shut with the metal clamps.

You must "burp" the jars daily, which means to open the jar, push down the kimchi under the liquid (brine), and allow any excess carbon dioxide to escape. I recommend taste testing daily to see how the flavor changes during the fermentation process. I can't help but eat some kimchi immediately after putting it together. I personally think the flavor is best on day 3 or 4, but I normally let it ferment 5 to 7 days until the cabbage begins to taste a bit sour. Store at room temperature, ideally between 60 to 75°F (15 to 23°C), and keep out of direct sunlight. Once fermentation is complete, store in an airtight container or jar and refrigerate.

RECIPE VARIATION

For a milder kimchi, follow the recipe above but omit the gochugaru (coarse hot pepper powder). I have made small batches of this non-spicy kimchi for my daughter to enjoy, occasionally adding in just 1 tablespoon of gochugaru for the slightest hint of spice.

NOTES

JACKFRUIT KIMCHI

This guest recipe has been created by Sarah Arrazola, founder of St. Pete Ferments located in St. Petersburg, Florida! She's inspired to ferment with what is locally in abundance each season. Sarah says, "Oh yeah, this is a hot one! When it has fermented to your liking, place it in the fridge and enjoy it for several months. A pale sherbet brine will form, a color reminiscent of a Florida sunset."

YIELD: I WECK quart jar (3–4 cups)

1 lb. napa cabbage, cut into bite-size
  pieces
⅓ cup jackfruit, cut into strips
⅓ cup daikon radishes, sliced
⅓ cup (skin on) carrots, sliced
2 green onions, chopped
1¼ tsp. kosher salt

PASTE:

3–4 garlic cloves
1–2 inches ginger root
2–3 habanero peppers

Clean the jackfruit. You may choose to wear gloves. I designate a special knife just for this fruit because of the tacky latex juice. I also find that cutting on a cardboard box helps to prevent countertop or other surface from staining. It sounds involved, but trust me, it is worth it. In a large nonreactive container such as a stainless-steel pot or glass bowl, combine the cabbage, jackfruit, radishes, carrots, and green onions with the salt. Massage all ingredients with your hands. Pour off excess brine if you wish; you should still have enough brine for the final product. In a food processor or other chopping device, blend all the kimchi paste ingredients. Wearing gloves, mix the paste well into the vegetable mixture. Transfer kimchi as well as all the natural brine into a clean quart WECK jar, pushing down the mixture to pack it into the jar. Leave 2 to 3 inches of headspace so the jars do not overflow during fermentation. Add the orange rubber WECK jar ring and lid, and secure shut with metal clamps.

You must "burp" the jar daily, which means to open the jar, push down the kimchi under the liquid (brine), and allow any excess carbon dioxide to escape. This is a 5- to 7-day ferment, depending on your personal taste. Store at room temperature, ideally between 60 to 75°F (15 to 23°C), and keep out of direct sunlight. Once fermentation is complete, store in an airtight container or jar and refrigerate.

NOTES

BRUSSELS SPROUT KIMCHI

These brussels sprouts will be tender and full of sour kimchi flavor once fermentation is complete. Enjoy them mixed into your favorite meals as you would traditional kimchi or eat them as a flavor-packed healthy snack.

YIELD: 1 WECK quart jar (3–4 cups)

4 cups brussels sprouts, ends trimmed, halved (if small) or quartered (if large)

KIMCHI BASE:

¼ cup onion

2 garlic cloves

1-inch ginger root, peeled

1 tsp. fish sauce (optional)

⅛–¼ cup gochugaru (coarse pepper powder)

chopped scallions (optional)

grated carrots (optional)

BRINE:

2 tsp. kosher salt dissolved in 2 cups water

Clean and prepare brussels sprouts by trimming ends and any flawed areas and removing outer layer of leaves. Set aside halved or quartered brussels sprouts in a large nonreactive bowl. Finely chop or use a food processor to purée the onion, garlic, ginger, and optional fish sauce. Add this mixture to a bowl and add in the coarse pepper powder and optional scallions and carrots; mix well. Combine the kimchi base with the brussels sprouts, mix together well, and transfer to a clean WECK jar. Pack the brussels sprouts into the jar well, trying not to leave any gaps of air within the vegetables.

Mix brine and pour over the brussels sprouts mixture as needed until all the brussels sprouts are covered. Use a smaller WECK jar lid or two as a weight to hold the veggies under the brine. Leave 1 to 2 inches of headspace for the brussels sprouts to ferment and bubble. Add the WECK jar ring and lid, and secure it shut by clipping on the metal clamps directly across from one another. Ferment at room temperature, ideally between 60 to 75°F (15 to 23°C), and keep out of direct sunlight.

This is a 7- to 10-day ferment. Check on the ferment every day to make sure the brine remains over the brussels sprouts. Open the jar daily to "burp" the ferment to allow the carbon dioxide to release, mix with a clean spoon, and pack it back into the jar. Once fermentation is complete, store in an airtight container or jar and refrigerate.

NOTES

PARSNIP PICKLES

So simple yet so delicious. These pickles can be added to salads, on sandwiches, and eaten as a side dish or as-is for a quick snack.

YIELD: 1 WECK pint jar (2 cups)

½ lb. parsnips, cut into ¼-inch coins
1 garlic clove, smashed

BRINE:

2 tsp. kosher salt dissolved in 1 cup
   water

Wash and prepare parsnips by trimming off the ends and coining; do not peel. Add the garlic to the bottom of the jar and fill with parsnips; pack them in tightly without bruising. Pour the brine over the parsnips until they are completely submerged. Leave 1½ inches of headspace for the weight, brine, and room for the ferment to bubble. Use a smaller WECK jar lid or two as a weight to hold the pickled parsnips underneath the brine. Add the WECK jar ring and lid, and secure it shut by adding the metal clamps directly across from one another. Ferment at room temperature, ideally between 60 to 75°F (15 to 23°C), and keep out of direct sunlight.

This is a 5- to 7-day ferment; taste test to determine completion. Open the jar daily to "burp" the ferment to allow the carbon dioxide to release. This may need to be done multiple times a day, as this is an active ferment. Make sure the brine remains over the parsnips. If the brine is low, use a clean finger or utensil to press down the weight to bring the brine back over the pickles. Once fermentation is complete, store in an airtight container or jar and refrigerate.

NOTES

PICKLED JALAPEÑOS

YIELD: I WECK pint jar (2 cups)

4 cloves of garlic, crushed
I grape leaf or other leaf with tannins
  (optional, to keep the veggies crunchy)
2 cups jalapeños, sliced ¼-inch thick

BRINE:

2 tsp. kosher salt dissolved in I cup
  water

Add the garlic to the bottom of a clean jar, and tuck the optional grape or other leaf on the side without breaking it. Pack the pepper slices in well, being mindful not to crush or damage them. Pour the brine over the peppers until they are completely submerged. Leave 1½ inches of headspace for the weight, brine, and room for the ferment to bubble. Use a smaller WECK jar lid or two as a weight to hold the peppers underneath the brine. Add the WECK jar ring and lid, and secure it shut by adding the metal clamps directly across from one another. Ferment at room temperature, ideally between 60 to 75°F (15 to 23°C), and keep out of direct sunlight.

This is a 5-day ferment. Be sure to "burp" the ferment daily to release any built-up carbon dioxide. If the peppers are above the brine, use a clean finger or utensil to press down the weight to bring the brine back over the ferment. Once fermentation is complete, store in an airtight container or jar and refrigerate.

NOTES

PICKLED RED ONIONS

These fermented onions are excellent for sandwiches (especially pulled pork or burgers), served over fish, added to salads, or used as a garnish!

YIELD: 1 WECK quart jar (4 cups)

½ tsp. whole black peppercorns

2 cloves garlic, crushed

1–2 large red onions, peeled and sliced ¼-inch thick

1 bay leaf

BRINE:

1 tbsp. salt dissolved in 2 cups water

Pack jar with peppercorns and garlic at the bottom, onions on top, and the bay leaf gently tucked on the side to avoid breakage. Pour the brine over the onions until they are completely submerged. Leave 1 to 2 inches of headspace for the weight, brine, and room for the ferment to bubble. Use a smaller WECK jar lid or two as a weight to hold the onions underneath the brine. Add the WECK jar ring and lid, and secure it shut by adding the metal clamps directly across from one another. Ferment at room temperature, ideally between 60 to 75°F (15 to 23°C), and keep out of direct sunlight.

This is a 7-day ferment. Check on the ferment every day to make sure the brine remains over the onions, and "burp" the ferment by allowing any built-up carbon dioxide to release. If the brine is low, use a clean finger or utensil to press down the weight to bring the brine back over the ferment. Once fermentation is complete, store in an airtight container or jar and refrigerate.

NOTES

SALSA

Salsa, oh, delicious salsa. It's good on everything—'nuff said.

YIELD: 1 WECK quart jar (3–4 cups)

3 ripe tomatoes, diced (3 cups)
1 cup (½ of 1 whole) onion, finely diced
¼ cup (1 whole) jalapeño, finely chopped
1 garlic clove, finely chopped
juice of 1 lime
¼ cup cilantro, chopped
½ tsp. kosher salt
ground black pepper, to taste

Prepare all ingredients and mix them together in a large nonreactive stainless-steel pot or glass bowl. Pack the mixture into a WECK quart-size jar. Use a smaller WECK jar lid or two as a weight to hold the salsa underneath the brine. Place the glass lid with rubber ring in place over the rim of the jar and carefully clip the two metal clamps on the jar, directly across from one another. Ferment at room temperature, ideally between 60 to 75°F (15 to 23°C), and keep out of direct sunlight.

This is a 12- to 48-hour ferment. It is delicious eaten immediately when mixed together (taste it!), though after 12 to 48 hours of fermentation, the ingredients meld and transform. If the brine is low, use a clean finger or utensil to press down the weight to bring the brine back over the ferment. Taste test to determine when it's finished fermenting to your liking. Once fermentation is complete, store in an airtight container or jar and refrigerate. This ferment is best if eaten within two weeks.

NOTES

SAUERKRAUT

Sauerkraut is one of the most iconic fermented foods out there. It's a staple of many people's diets around the world. If everyone knew how easy it was to make themselves, they would never buy it from the store again. If you love making homemade sauerkraut as much as I do, I highly recommend purchasing a cabbage shredder or hunting one down at a garage sale. It turns a normally 30-minute chore into a 3- or 4-minute task. Not only does it speed up the process enormously, it shreds the cabbage perfectly for sauerkraut or coleslaw.

YIELD: **2–3 WECK quart jars (8–10 cups)**

2 heads (5 lb.) organic cabbage

2–3 tbsp. kosher salt

Remove the outer leaves from the cabbage and discard. Wash the cabbages with cold water. Cut each cabbage in half lengthwise and remove the core from each half. Shred the cabbages into thinly sliced pieces, about ⅛–¼-inch thick. Once all the cabbage is shredded, put the shreds in a large nonreactive bowl such as glass or stainless-steel. Mix the salt in with the cabbage shreds and massage the salt into the shreds. Once you are able to squeeze a handful of cabbage and liquid drips away, transfer the mixture into quart-size WECK jars.

Push down the cabbage mixture as you pack each vessel. I recommend using a stainless-steel funnel when transferring the shreds into the jars, as it limits the mess. I have a wooden kraut pounder (also known as a cabbage tamper or masher) for this task. The kraut pounder helps me get leverage and I'm able to pack the jars tightly while releasing the liquid from the cabbage, though clean fists and fingers work just as well. Pour any remaining brine from the bowl into the jars, leaving 1 to 2 inches of headspace. If there is not enough brine to cover the cabbage after an hour or so, mix extra brine (dissolve 1 tbsp. salt with 2 cups water) and add it to the jar until the cabbage shreds are covered. Use a glass lid or two from a smaller WECK jar as a weight to hold the cabbage underneath the brine. Add the rubber ring and lid, and clamp each WECK jar shut, or cover jar with cheesecloth or another breathable cover to keep dust and bugs from entering your ferment.

Whether you are using a cloth to cover this ferment, or closing it up with a glass lid, be sure to check on the ferment every day to make sure the brine remains over the cabbage and that no mold has begun to grow. If you are closing the lid on this ferment, be sure to "burp" it 1 to 2 times a day to release the built-up carbon dioxide. It is completely normal to see little bubbles or even foam-like bubbling occur at the top of the ferment. If the brine is low, use clean fingers or a utensil to press down the weight(s) to bring the brine back over the cabbage. Ferment at room temperature, ideally between 60 to 75°F (15 to 23°C), and keep out of direct sunlight. This is a 2- to 4-week ferment. Weekly taste testing is recommended to determine which flavor you prefer as the ferment changes throughout the process. Once fermentation is complete, store in an airtight container or jar and refrigerate.

RECIPE VARIATIONS

Sauerkraut is so much fun to experiment with. Try adding caraway seeds, dried juniper berries, lemon, ginger, coriander seeds, or dill to your cabbage. Each ingredient adds a new flavor.

NOTES

_____
_____
_____
_____
_____

TURMERIC AND GARLIC SAUERKRAUT

YIELD: 1 WECK pint jar (2 cups)

½ head green cabbage
1 tsp. ground organic turmeric powder
2 garlic cloves, finely chopped

Follow the directions for making Sauerkraut (pg. 134), and once the cabbage shreds have been salted and are ready to pack into jars, add turmeric and garlic to the mixture. Mix well and follow the rest of the recipe directions for packing sauerkraut.

RED OR PURPLE SAUERKRAUT

YIELD: 1 WECK pint jar (2 cups)

½ head various colored cabbages
1 beet, grated (optional)

To make beautiful red or purple kraut, follow the directions for making Sauerkraut (pg. 134) but use various colored cabbages! Just prepare for blue fingers when making purple kraut. Adding one small grated beet (ends trimmed, skin on) to green cabbage will also create a beautiful pinkish-purple kraut and result in a slight earthy flavor.

NOTES

GUT SHOTS

If you have any brine leftover from your vegetable ferments, don't toss it—drink it! That leftover juice is what is popularly known as a "gut shot." It's filled with lots of probiotics, vitamin C, said to be a hangover cure, and heck, it tastes surprisingly good. If you aren't a fan of drinking the brine, use it as a marinade or to make a delicious salad dressing—just don't waste it!

FIERY CIDER SAUERKRAUT

This recipe was created by Wendy and Sue of NW Ferments. They are Oregon-based friends with a passion for fermented foods. They grow and sell starter cultures as well as fermentation supplies through their website and at natural food stores throughout the country. Their goal is to share their love of fermentation by helping folks "get fermented!" Wendy and Sue say, "This recipe includes all the immune-boosting benefits of 'fire cider' in a delicious, spicy kraut. A cup a day will help keep the cooties away! The ingredients of this recipe can be increased or decreased according to taste—the fierier, the better!"

YIELD: 1 WECK quart jar (3–4 cups)

6 cups (1 medium whole) cabbage, thinly sliced

2 cloves garlic, minced

1 jalapeño, minced

2 tsp. burdock root, minced or grated

1 tsp. ginger root, minced or grated

4 tsp. horseradish root, minced or grated

3 tsp. turmeric root, minced or grated

1 cup onion, thinly sliced

½ cup carrot, grated or thinly sliced

1 tbsp. kosher salt

Combine all the prepped vegetables in a large nonreactive stainless-steel or glass bowl. Sprinkle with ½ tbsp. salt and mix well to incorporate the salt throughout. Let sit for 30 minutes at room temperature. After resting, add the remaining ½ tbsp. salt and mix well. Let sit for another 30 minutes to allow the vegetables to release some of their juices, making your job a little easier. When the juices begin to accumulate in the bottom of the bowl, use a kraut pounder or clean hands to crush and gently squeeze the vegetables to create as much liquid (natural brine) as possible. Once plenty of juices have developed, pack the vegetables into your WECK jar. Use a cabbage pounder or your fist to tamp them down until the vegetables are completely covered with liquid. If there isn't enough natural brine to cover the produce completely, some brine can be added to top it off (1 tbsp. salt dissolved in 2 cups water); add more brine as needed. Place a smaller WECK jar lid or two as a weight to hold the veggies under the brine. Cover your jar securely with a WECK jar ring and lid, and clamp it shut.

Be sure to "burp" the jar daily to allow carbon dioxide to escape, and push the weight down to keep the brine above the ferment. Allow to ferment at room temperature—65 to 75°F (15 to 23°C) is ideal—for 5 to 7 days. Taste test the ferment after 4 days to check texture; the kraut is ready when it has softened a bit but still has some crunch to it. Once fermentation is complete, store in an airtight container or jar and refrigerate (unless you choose to eat it all right away!).

NOTES

SAUERRÜBEN

Sauerrüben is a traditional German sour ferment that is similar to sauerkraut, but it is a much shorter ferment and root vegetables are used in place of cabbage.

YIELD: 1 WECK quart jar (3–4 cups)

1 lb. (2–3 large) turnips
1 lb. (1–2 small) rutabagas
1 tbsp. kosher salt

Ingredient Variations:

As with sauerkraut, this ferment can be tweaked to your liking by adding in other vegetables such as carrots, or additional seasonings such as caraway seeds or a bay leaf.

Wash vegetables, trim off the ends, and leave the skin on. Grate veggies into a nonreactive stainless-steel or glass bowl. Add salt and mix well. After liquid has begun to release from the veggies (this could take several minutes up to an hour depending on freshness of veggies), transfer the sauerrüben as well as all the natural brine into a clean WECK jar. Push down the veggies and pack it well into the jar, using your fist or a cabbage tamper, and leave 1 inch of headspace so the jar does not overflow during fermentation. Use a glass lid or two from a smaller WECK jar as a weight to hold the ferment under the brine. Add the WECK jar ring and lid, and secure it shut by adding the metal clamps directly across from one another.

You must "burp" the jars daily, which means to open the jar, push down the veggies under the brine, and allow any excess carbon dioxide to escape. I recommend taste testing daily to see how the flavor changes during the fermentation process. This is a 5- to 7-day ferment. Store at room temperature, ideally between 60 to 75°F (15 to 23°C), and keep out of direct sunlight. Once fermentation is complete, store in an airtight container or jar and refrigerate.

RECIPE VARIATION

Try making sauerrüben with 2 lbs. rutabagas instead of half turnips and half rutabagas. It's one of my favorite, quick, kraut-like ferments.

NOTES

SOOTHING LEMON-GINGER SYRUP

I've been mixing up this concoction for years. I start it in the fall and use it as needed all winter long. I prefer to mix it into a mug of warm water or tea, but it can certainly be used in cooking or eaten by the spoonful.

YIELD: 1 WECK jam jar

1 organic lemon, sliced, seeds removed
1 tbsp. (2-inch chunk) fresh ginger root, finely grated
raw local honey, as needed to fill jar

Wash and prepare the lemon and add lemon slices and grated ginger to a clean jar. Pour in honey until the ingredients are completely covered, leaving 1-inch of headspace. Add the WECK jar ring and lid, and secure it shut by adding the metal clamps directly across from one another.

You must "burp" the jar daily, which means to open the lid and push the lemon slices down under the honey. Store at room temperature, ideally between 60 to 75°F (15 to 23°C), and keep out of direct sunlight. Over the next couple of days, the honey should become very watered down. At this point, store the syrup in the refrigerator in an airtight container. Use as needed.

NOTES

STRAWBERRY CHUTNEY

This fermented delight is a treat for the taste buds. It pairs well with spicy proteins such as grilled jerk chicken or spicy marinated tofu but can also double as a delicious condiment for cheese and crackers.

YIELD: I WECK pint (2 cups)

2 cups fresh organic strawberries, stems removed

1 cup (½ of 1 whole) red onion

¼ cup red or golden raisins

¼ cup dried apricots

1 tbsp. (1-inch chunk) fresh ginger root, peeled

1 garlic clove

1 tbsp. raw local honey

2 tsp. organic apple cider vinegar

½ tsp. kosher salt

Put all ingredients into a food processor and pulse until it reaches a chunky, sauce-like consistency. Transfer the mixture to a clean WECK jar. Add the glass lid with rubber ring in place over the rim of the jar and carefully attach the two metal clamps on the jar directly across from one another. Open the jar once daily to stir mixture. Ferment at room temperature, ideally between 60 to 75°F (15 to 23°C), and keep out of direct sunlight.

Fermentation duration is between 2 to 4 days. I recommend taste testing daily to see how the flavor changes during the fermentation process. Once fermentation is complete, store in an airtight container or jar and refrigerate. This ferment will last up to 2 weeks refrigerated.

NOTES

SHRUBS

Shrubs are homemade drinks that are essentially syrup made of fresh fruit and sugar that is mixed with vinegar. The possibilities are endless when it comes to what concoctions can be created. Shrubs can be enjoyed over ice, mixed with bubbly water, or used to make a zingy cocktail. Below I explain the most flavorful and easiest process for making a shrub, also commonly referred to as a "drinking vinegar."

YIELD: 1 WECK pint (2 cups)

1½ cups chopped fruit of choice
herbs (optional)
1½ cups organic or non-GMO
  granulated sugar or other
  natural sweetener of choice
1½ cups organic apple cider
  vinegar or other vinegar of
  choice

Combine fruit(s), optional herbs, and sugar or other natural sweetener of choice and mix well. Add mixture to WECK jar and cover with rubber ring and lid and clamp it shut. Leave the jar on the counter at room temperature for 3 to 4 days until the natural juices separate from the fruit and mix with the sugar to create a syrup. Stir the fruit and sugar mixture several times a day, if able; this will help speed up the syrup-making process. If using solid fruits such as blueberries, use a clean spoon to break them down a bit so the natural juices are released and mix with the sugar. Frozen fruits are great options, too, since the juices are more readily available once thawed.

After a few days, when the sugar and fruit has mixed together to create a syrup, use a fine mesh strainer to strain out the solids, reserving the fruit syrup in a clean jar. Then, add vinegar of equal measurement to the amount of syrup made, and mix well. I prefer to mix the fruit syrup with apple cider vinegar in my shrubs, not only because of the probiotic benefit, but because I consider it to have the best flavor. However, wine vinegar, white distilled vinegar, or any other vinegar that is at least 5 percent acidity can be used in its place! Store in an airtight container or jar and refrigerate. Drink within a few months for best flavor. To serve, I like to mix 2 ounces of completed shrub with 6 ounces of tap water and drink it from a pretty glass filled with ice.

RECIPE VARIATION

Honey, brown sugar, coconut sugar, or even maple syrup can be substituted for sugar in this recipe.

NOTES

GET CREATIVE!

If you can dream it, you can make it! Fruits such as blackberries, peaches, pears, grapefruit, strawberries, raspberries, pomegranates, and blueberries; herbs such as rosemary, lavender, basil; or even seasonings such as cardamom, cinnamon stick, and vanilla bean make a delicious and unique shrub. Keep notes of your concoctions so you can duplicate the blends you enjoy most!

MIX UP A COCKTAIL!

If you want to make a delicious thirst-quenching cocktail on a hot summer's day, try mixing one-part whiskey, rum, or vodka with 3 parts switchel; stir and serve over ice.

SWITCHEL

A drink once best-known to be a thirst-quencher for the American farmer is now making its way onto grocery store shelves. There is debate around the origination of switchel, but vinegar drinks have been noted around the world for centuries. Its potassium-dense ingredients offer electrolytes, which make this a perfectly hydrating drink. I prefer switchel best when served over ice.

YIELD: 1 WECK pint jar (2 cups)

1 tbsp. fresh ginger root, peeled and grated or finely chopped
1 tbsp. apple cider vinegar
2 cups water
1–2 tbsp. raw local honey

Mix together ginger, vinegar, water, and honey until the honey is dissolved. Cover with the WECK jar ring and lid, secure tightly with clamps. Allow mixture to ferment for 24 hours. Refrigerate after completion.

If the ginger flavor is too prevalent for your liking, add a little extra water to your cup when serving to dilute the intensity. In contrast, if you want a more intense ginger flavor, consider adding 2 tbsp. in your next batch!

RECIPE VARIATION

Use organic maple syrup or blackstrap molasses in place of honey for an alternative sweetener; each offers a delicious and unique outcome. Consider muddling in some of your favorite fresh herbs to alter the flavor, or even a cinnamon stick.

NOTES

TABLE-RADISH PICKLES

Fermented radishes are one of my favorite ferments. They are incredibly easy to make and fermentation process completely changes the flavor; the intensity of the raw radish is entirely softened. If you don't like radishes in their natural state, you may enjoy them after their fermented transformation. They are great added to pretty much anything: salads, sandwiches, pickle platters, or just eaten as a quick snack!

YIELD: **1 WECK pint jar (2 cups)**

2 cups radishes, sliced

1 garlic clove, crushed

BRINE:

2 tsp. kosher salt dissolved in 1 cup water

Wash and prepare radishes by trimming off the ends before slicing. Add the garlic to the bottom of the jar first, then fill with radish slices; pack them in tightly without crushing or breaking them. Pour the brine over the radish slices until they are completely submerged. Leave 1½ inches of headspace for the weight, brine, and room for the ferment to bubble. Use a smaller WECK jar lid or two as a weight to hold the radish slices under the brine. Add the WECK jar ring and lid, and secure it shut by adding the metal clamps directly across from one another.

Ferment at room temperature, ideally between 60 to 75°F (15 to 23°C), and keep out of direct sunlight. This is a 5- to 7-day ferment; taste test to determine completion. Open the jar one or more times daily to "burp" the ferment to allow the carbon dioxide to release. Check to make sure the brine remains over the radish slices. If the brine is low, use a clean finger or utensil to press down the weight to bring the brine back over the ferment. Once fermentation is complete, store in an airtight container or jar and refrigerate.

NOTES

THYME AND LEEK PASTE

This guest recipe comes from Cali-born, Vancouver Island, British Columbia transplant, Holly Howe—blog owner of MakeSauerkraut.com. She is known for using unexpected ingredients in her kraut, such as pineapple and lime zest, to entice the palate. Holly says, "This paste is a savory mix of leeks and herbs, fermented in its own brine. Use it to enhance the flavor of soups, stews, sautéed greens, and pasta dishes. It's also a delicious spread for cheese and crackers or on a turkey sandwich."

YIELD: I WECK pint jar (2 cups)

2–3 (1 lb.) leeks, grit removed, coarsely
  chopped
3 garlic cloves
2–3 tsp. kosher salt
1 tsp. dried sage
1 tsp. dried thyme

Wash and prepare leeks by removing the tough outer leaves and cutting off the darkest portion of each stalk. Slice lengthwise into uniform-size pieces. Rinse under cold water, removing any dirt. In a food processor, pulse the garlic until finely chopped, then add leeks and pulse again until roughly chopped. Add in 2 tsp. salt, 1 tsp. dried sage, and 1 tsp. dried thyme and pulse until the mixture is smooth. Taste test to determine if more salt is desired, if so, add remaining 1 tsp. salt. Pack mixture into a clean WECK jar, leaving 1 to 2 inches of headspace. Push it down well to remove any pockets of air trapped within the jar. If there is additional paste, pack it into a smaller jar to ferment. Add the glass WECK lid with rubber ring in place over the rim of the jar and carefully attach the two metal clamps on the jar directly across from one another.

Ferment at room temperature, ideally between 60 to 75°F (15 to 23°C), and keep out of direct sunlight. Fermentation duration is between 3 to 5 days. Open the jar once daily to stir mixture. Taste the paste at day 4 to determine if it's finished fermenting; it should taste slightly sour. It's ready when the bright green of the leeks has dulled, and the leeks have softened. Once fermentation is complete, store in an airtight container or jar and refrigerate. The flavor will continue to change while refrigerated.

NOTES

ABOUT INFUSED SPIRITS

Infusing alcohol with fruit when it's at its peak is a tasty way to preserve the flavors of the season, as well as experiment with new flavor combinations. WECK juice jars are ideal for this task because not only are they pretty, they are also the perfect size for a small batch of infused booze. Plus, the shape of WECK juice jars helps keep chunks of fruit under the neck of the jar. For the most part, all you need to create your own alcohol infusions are ripe fruit, whichever alcohol you want to infuse, and a jar. It's that easy! Well, and generally a couple of weeks (or months) of time.

I largely stick to the rule of 1 cup of fruit for every 2 cups of alcohol. Be sure to use clean jars and fresh fruit without bruising or flaws (frozen fruit works as well, but fresh is always preferred). Pour 2 cups of alcohol over the fruit. I generally use a mid-level, mid-price liquor (generally what I'd normally buy to mix cocktails with) and my infusions have always turned out great. Once you've combined the fruit and alcohol, just clamp the rubber ring and lid onto the jars securely and leave out of direct sunlight. You'll notice over time that the fruit will become pale and lose color; that's because the flavors and color are being pulled out of the fruit and infused with the alcohol. I allow the flavors to mix for at least 2 weeks before tasting (except for hot pepper infusions; those are ready after just a few days).

Once the infusion is complete, you can strain the fruit solids out or leave the fruit in—it's up to you—and reserve the flavored alcohol. I tend to do both, depending on the infusion. Strawberries tend to look white and unappetizing after soaking in alcohol, but the pinkish-red liquor left behind is gorgeous.

I recommend tasting your infusions often. If after 3 days you are pleased with the flavor, strain out the solids at that point. If you don't feel it has enough flavor, let it keep going and taste again in a few days. From my personal experience, I think the infusions tend to get better and better with time. I leave much of the fruit in my infusions indefinitely. The flavor after 6 months is usually better than at 2 weeks.

To strain out solids, use a fine mesh strainer. If you are still seeing bits of solids floating in the liquor, try straining it through again or line the strainer with cheesecloth or a coffee filter to catch more of the solids. Once the infusion is complete, it should be left at room temperature and kept out of direct sunlight. Infusions can also be refrigerated if you prefer your spirits chilled.

Label each infused jar with the liquor type and ingredients and start date for quick reference.

BOOZY INFUSIONS

Brandy

161

APRICOT

CHERRY

CRANBERRY

Vodka

162

APPLE-CINNAMON-VANILLA

CHERRY

CRANBERRY

CUCUMBER-BASIL

JALAPEÑO-HABANERO

LEMON

MANGO

MANGO-HABANERO

ORANGE

ORANGE-CLOVE-CINNAMON

ORANGE-LEMON

ORANGE-VANILLA

PEACH

PINEAPPLE

PINEAPPLE-MANGO

PINEAPPLE-STRAWBERRY

STRAWBERRY

VANILLA

Whiskey

165

APPLE-CINNAMON-VANILLA

CHERRY

CRANBERRY

ORANGE-CLOVE-CINNAMON

PEACH

PEAR

STRAWBERRY

Gin

166

BLACKBERRY

GRAPEFRUIT

LEMON

LIME

MINT

STRAWBERRY

Rum

169

WHITE RUM:

MANGO

PINEAPPLE

DARK RUM:

PINEAPPLE

TOASTED COCONUT

Tequila

170

JALAPEÑO-HABANERO

LIME

PEPPERCORNS

PINEAPPLE

BRANDY

YIELD: **WECK** juice jar

1 cup fruit of choice
2 cups brandy

INFUSED FRUIT OPTIONS:

- apricot, dried or fresh, pitted
- cherry, pitted

RECIPE VARIATION

Because cranberries are bitter and have a firm skin, there is an extra step you must take when infusing with them. In a small saucepan, heat 2 tbsp. organic granulated sugar and 2 tbsp. water and mix until the sugar has dissolved. Add in 1 cup rinsed cranberries and stir well. Allow them to cook 1 to 2 minutes, just until they begin to pop and split, then remove from heat. Allow them to cool and mix them and the sugar syrup together with the alcohol.

NOTES

VODKA

YIELD: **WECK** juice jar

1 cup fruit of choice
2 cups vodka

INFUSED FLAVOR OPTIONS:

apple-cinnamon-vanilla: 3 slices dehydrated apple, 1 cinnamon stick, and ½ vanilla bean (sliced lengthwise)	**cherry:** pitted, halved	**cucumber-basil:** 1 cup sliced cucumbers, 5 fresh basil leaves (this is a much shorter infusion and tastes great with Bloody Marys; infuse about 5 days)	**lemon:** peel of ½ lemon, no pith, washed, un-waxed
mango	**jalapeño-habanero:** ½ jalapeño pepper, ½ habanero pepper (this is a quicker infusion; taste after just a few days)	**mango-habanero:** 1 cup fresh mango, ½ habanero pepper	**orange:** peel of ½ orange, no pith, washed, un-waxed
orange-clove-cinnamon: dehydrated orange slices, 1 whole clove, and 1 whole cinnamon stick	**orange-lemon:** peel of ½ lemon, no pith, washed, un-waxed and peel of ½ orange, no pith, washed, un-waxed	**orange-vanilla:** dehydrated orange slices, 1 whole vanilla bean (sliced lengthwise)	**peach:** pitted and sliced
pineapple: cut into chunks	**pineapple-mango:** ½ cup of each	**pineapple-strawberry:** ½ cup of each	**strawberry:** stems removed, halved
vanilla: ½ vanilla bean, halved lengthwise			

RECIPE VARIATION

Because cranberries are bitter and have a firm skin, there is an extra step you must take when infusing with them. In a small saucepan, heat 2 tbsp. organic granulated sugar and 2 tbsp. water and mix until the sugar has dissolved. Add in 1 cup rinsed cranberries and stir well. Allow them to cook 1 to 2 minutes, just until they begin to pop and split, then remove from heat. Allow them to cool and mix them and the sugar syrup together with the alcohol.

NOTES

WHISKEY

YIELD: **WECK** juice jar

1 cup fruit of choice
2 cups whiskey

INFUSED FLAVOR OPTIONS:

* apple-cinnamon-vanilla: dehydrated apple slices, 1 cinnamon stick, and 1 whole vanilla bean
* cherry: pitted and halved
* orange-clove-cinnamon: dehydrated orange slices, 1 whole clove, and 1 whole cinnamon stick
* peach: pitted and sliced
* pear: cored and sliced
* strawberry: stems removed, halved

RECIPE VARIATION

Because cranberries are bitter and have a firm skin, there is an extra step you must take when infusing with them. In a small saucepan, heat 2 tbsp. organic granulated sugar and 2 tbsp. water and mix until the sugar has dissolved. Add in 1 cup rinsed cranberries and stir well. Allow them to cook 1 to 2 minutes, just until they begin to pop and split, then remove from heat. Allow them to cool and mix them and the sugar syrup together with the alcohol.

NOTES

GIN

YIELD: **WECK** juice jar

1 cup fruit of choice
2 cups gin

INFUSED FLAVOR OPTIONS:

- blackberry: fresh, gently muddled
- grapefruit: peel of ¼ grapefruit, no pith, washed, un-waxed
- lemon: peel of ½ lemon, no pith, washed, un-waxed
- lime: peel of ½ lime, no pith, washed, un-waxed
- mint: fresh mint leaves (this is a quicker infusion, taste after just a few days)
- strawberry: stems removed, halved

NOTES

RUM

YIELD: WECK juice jar

1 cup fruit of choice
2 cups rum

White Rum:

- mango: cut into chunks
- pineapple: cut into chunks

Dark Rum:

- pineapple: cut into chunks
- toasted coconut: 1 cup dried toasted coconut flakes (to toast the coconut, bake in the oven at 350°F for 10 minutes or so until the flakes begin to brown. Remove from oven and allow them to cool before mixing with the rum).

NOTES

TEQUILA

YIELD: **WECK** juice jar

1 cup fruit of choice
2 cups tequila

INFUSED FLAVOR OPTIONS:

- jalapeño-habanero: 1 jalapeño pepper, sliced and ½ habanero pepper, sliced
- lime: peel of ½ lime, no pith, washed, un-waxed
- peppercorns
- pineapple, cut into chunks

NOTES

PART III

Blanching Times for Vegetables

VEGETABLE	TIME* in minutes
Asparagus, medium	2
Beans, green and wax	3
Beans, lima and pinto	3
Broccoli florets	3
Brussels sprouts	4
Cabbage, shredded	1½
Carrots, sliced	2
Cauliflower, florets	3
Corn	5–6
Eggplant	4
Kohlrabi, cubed	1
Okra, medium	3
Peas, edible pod	2
Potatoes	3–5
Summer Squash	3
Turnips, cubed	2

*Blanching times given are for boiling-water blanching method. Double the time if using a steam method for blanching.

FREEZING WITH WECK®

WECK jars are great for freezing fruits and vegetables! The jars keep an airtight seal which defers freezer burn. It is recommended to use the style of jars with the straight sides (mold-style), with wide mouth openings. WECK also offers "Keep Fresh" lids, which they recommend for freezing foods. Please remember that food expands when it is frozen, so it is important to leave proper of headspace to avoid breakage. It is also necessary to avoid extreme changes in temperature, so be sure that all hot foods are completely cooled before freezing. Here are some tips for freezing fruits and vegetables, provided by WECK:

Freezing Fruits

Syrup Pack: Dissolve 1-part sugar in 2 parts water, then chill. Pack fruit into jars and pour syrup over fruit. Leave ½ inch of headspace for ¼ liter (1 cup) and ½ liter (2 cups = pint) jars and 1 inch of headspace for 1-liter (4 cups = quart) jars. Clip shut jar with rubber ring, lid, and clamps or add "Keep Fresh" lid.

Sugar Pack: Coat fruit pieces with sugar, then pack into jars using ½ inch of headspace. Clip jar shut with rubber ring, lid, and clamps or add "Keep Fresh" lid.

Tray Pack, a.k.a. "IQF: Individually Quick Frozen": Freeze fruit on a tray for 1 hour, then pack into jars. Very little headspace is needed in this case, as the fruit is already frozen. Clip jar shut with rubber ring, lid, and clamps or add "Keep Fresh" lid.

Freezing Vegetables

- Wash and strain vegetables before removing skins or hulls. Cut into pieces if necessary.
- Blanch vegetables before freezing to inactivate enzymes. Use 1 gallon of water for 1 lb. of vegetables. Follow times in blanching chart (pg. 174).
- Chill vegetables in ice water for same time as blanching time, then drain or allow to dry on lint-free towels.

Packing Vegetables

Dry Pack: Pack vegetables into jars leaving ½ inch of headspace. Clip jar shut with rubber ring, lid, and clamps or add "Keep Fresh" lid.

Tray Pack (IQF): Freeze vegetable pieces for 1 hour, then pack into jars. Very little headspace is needed since the vegetables are already frozen. Clip shut jar with rubber ring, lid, and clamps or add "Keep Fresh" lid.

TROUBLESHOOTING

A water-bath canned jar did not seal or unsealed after storage.

Very rarely will a jar not seal. This is likely due to a faulty rubber ring or a defect in the rim of the jar. Perhaps there was a chip or crack that was not noticed before processing.

If a jar becomes unsealed after processing, chances are that the preserve was not properly processed. If the water bath did not reach a boil for 10 minutes or more—time varies per recipe—the bacteria in the canned food may not have been killed, therefore the gasses within the preserve will have pushed the lid off the sealed jar. This is meant as a safety warning for you to detect preserves that are unsafe to eat. All contents should be discarded if this occurs.

Other signs that a canned good has spoiled: foul odor, slime, mold, or bubbling (fermentation).

The fermented food is cloudy.

The brine of a ferment will become cloudy; this is part of the process of fermentation and an indication that things are going exactly as they should.

My ferment is moldy.

It is crucial that you keep all veggies underneath the brine to keep them safe from the air. If a piece of cabbage is poking out of the brine, it is susceptible to mold. That is why I recommend checking on the ferments daily to make sure everything is looking and smelling good, that all the veggies are under the brine, and that there is no sign of kahm yeast or mold.

My fermenting jars are overflowing.

It is totally normal for a very active ferment to overflow a bit. This can be curbed by leaving proper headspace, "burping" your ferment daily to release any gas build-up, and pushing the produce back down if it has risen due to carbon dioxide build-up. If a ferment seems more active than others, burp it 2 to 3 times a day. You can also put the jar in a bowl or tray to catch any overflow instead of making a fer-*mess*. Otherwise, remove some of the fermenting produce and add it to another jar so each jar can have 1 to 2 inches of headspace, as needed.

Why did the garlic turn green?

Occasionally garlic turns green or blue during fermentation and canning. This is nothing to worry about; it's a natural chemical reaction that can occur.

OTHER USES FOR WECK® JARS

- Candle holder
- Craft storage (beads, decorative tapes, beads, scrapbooking supplies, etc.)
- Dessert dishware
- Drinking glasses
- Flower vase
- Homemade bath salts or sugar scrubs
- Homemade lotion or candle storage
- Homemade terrariums
- Leftover food storage
- Lids can be used as a tea-light holder
- Pantry organization for dried foods
- One-serving desserts
- Salad to-go
- Salt or seasoning storage jars
- Yogurt parfait to-go

RESOURCES

The J. WECK® Company: weckjars.com

Shop online for a complete selection of WECK jars, replacement lids, rubber rings, metal clasps, and other WECK home preservation supplies.

WECK® Jar Suppliers:

Amazon.com
Container Store: containerstore.com
Cost Plus World Market
Crate & Barrel: crateandbarrel.com
Food52.com
Heath Ceramics: heathceramics.com
School House Electric & Supply Co.: schoolhouse.com
Terrain: shopterrain.com
The Container Store: containerstore.com
Williams Sonoma: williams-sonoma.com
World Market: worldmarket.com

Canning Crafts Labels: canningcrafts.com

Sign up for their newsletter to save 10% on your first order!
Gorgeous jar labels and tags, completely customizable.

National Center for Home Preservation: http://nchfp.uga.edu

A wonderful resource of research-based recommendations for most methods of home food preservation.

NW Ferments: nwferments.com

To save 10% on your next order, use promo code: CULTURE
A great resource for fermentation supplies such as starter cultures for home production, as well as airlocks, salt, and more.

Stone Creek Trading: stonecreektrading.com

To save $5 on orders over $50, use PROMO CODE: WECK5
A great resource for fermentation-related supplies such as crocks, weights, cabbage shredders, cabbage pounders, and more.

Wild Fermentation: wildfermentation.com

Sandor Katz's website includes links to his books which go in depth about the process and history of fermentation, as well as recipes for fermented vegetables, cheese, yogurt, bread, and more.

FROM THE KITCHEN OF
STEPHANIE

FROM THE KITCHEN OF
STEPHANIE

FROM THE KITCHEN OF
STEPHANIE

FROM THE KITCHEN OF
STEPHANIE

FROM THE KITCHEN OF
STEPHANIE

FROM THE KITCHEN OF
STEPHANIE

ABOUT THE AUTHOR

Stephanie Thurow first learned the kitchen craft of water-bath canning in the early 2000s. What initially started as a mission to make the perfect garlic dill pickle quickly morphed into a way of life. She finds great pride in canning and fermenting fresh, organic produce that can be preserved for year-round enjoyment and shared with her loved ones. She enjoys teaching others how to cook and preserve from scratch and wants to empower people to try their hand at preserving. Her non-intimidating approach to home preservation puts even a novice at ease.

Stephanie's first cookbook, *Can It & Ferment It* (2017), brings the canning and fermenting communities together by offering recipes that work for both canning and fermenting. Readers will learn how to preserve each fruit and vegetable in two different ways; each can be enjoyed water-bath canned or as a healthy, probiotic-rich ferment. Recipes are organized by season.

Connect with Stephanie

Minnesota from Scratch Blog: minnesotafromscratch.com
Instagram: @minnesotafromscratch
Twitter: @StephLovestoCan
Facebook: facebook.com/MinnesotaFromScratch/

Turn the page for some of my favorite recipes!

BONUS RECIPES

APPLESAUCE

This is an extremely simple recipe that yields a delicious fermented applesauce.

YIELD: 1 WECK pint jar

3 organic apples, cored and rough-chopped

⅛ tsp. kosher salt

½ tsp. ground cinnamon (optional)

Put apples into a food processor and purée until apples are broken down into a smooth applesauce consistency. I like to leave the skins on, but removing the skins before puréeing will result in a smoother applesauce. Transfer applesauce into a clean WECK pint-sized jar and stir in salt and optional cinnamon, if desired. Mix well. Cover the WECK jar with the rubber ring and glass lid, and clamp it shut. Ferment at room temperature, ideally between 60 to 75°F (15 to 23°C), and keep out of direct sunlight.

Check on the ferment once a day by removing the lid and stirring the applesauce, placing the lid back on, and clamping shut. Keep ferment out of direct sunlight or wrap a dish towel around the jar to keep light out. This is a 3-day ferment. Refrigerate for up to 2 weeks.

NOTES

GREEN TOMATO SALSA

Tearing down the garden at the end of the season won't be as disappointing when you have this salsa to look forward to, made from unripe tomatoes. Use this salsa as you would any traditional red tomato salsa.

YIELD: 1 WECK quart jar

6 cups fresh green tomatoes
½ onion, yellow or purple
2 jalapeños
½ cup cilantro
1 ½ tsp. salt
Fresh lime juice, for serving

If using a food processor, add all the ingredients except the salt and lime. Pulse in food processor a couple of times until the tomatoes are broken down to a salsa consistency. If you do not have access to a food processor, dice the green tomatoes and finely chop the other ingredients by hand. Transfer to a nonreactive bowl, mix in the salt, and stir well.

Transfer salsa to a quart jar and add the WECK jar ring and lid, and clamp it shut. Burp the ferment 1 to 2 times a day; stir up the ferment and press it back down, allowing the carbon dioxide to release. Ferment at room temperature, ideally between 60 to 75°F (15 to 23°C), and keep out of direct sunlight.

This salsa is excellent freshly made! As with all ferments, the flavors change during the fermentation process. Taste after 24 hours, again after 48 hours, etc. to determine when it's done to your liking. I ferment this recipe for 3 days.

Mix in freshly squeezed lime juice to salsa before serving. Store in an airtight container after fermentation is complete and refrigerate. Best if eaten within 2 weeks.

NOTES

PINEAPPLE ZUCCHINI

This recipe was adapted from one on the National Center for Home Food Preservation website when I was looking for a new way to use up excess zucchini. After preservation, the shredded zucchini tastes just like crushed pineapple and can be substituted in recipes that call for regular crushed pineapple.

YIELD: **3 WECK** jam jars (3 cups)

4½ cups (2–3 small to medium) zucchini, peeled, shredded
1½ cups unsweetened pineapple juice
½ cup lemon juice
¾ cup sugar

Wash, peel, and shred the zucchini. Use a potato peeler to remove the skin. You may need to peel it twice to get all of the green tint removed from the zucchini. Add zucchini and all other ingredients to a heavy-bottomed saucepan and bring to a boil. Let mixture simmer for 25 minutes, stirring often to avoid burning.

Ladle the hot mixture into prepared jars. Use a funnel to safely transfer the hot pineapple-zucchini mix into jars. Leave ½ inch of headspace. Wipe the rims of the jars with a dampened, clean, lint-free cloth or paper towel and again with a dry towel. Place a glass lid with rubber ring in place over the rim of each jar and carefully clip the two metal clamps on each jar, one directly across from another. Process in the water bath for 15 minutes. Carefully remove jars from the water bath with canning tongs and place the jars on a towel for 12 hours without touching. Store in the refrigerator after breaking the seal.

RECIPE VARIATION

Follow the directions referenced above, but instead of shredding the zucchini, remove the seeds and cut them into chunks.

NOTES

WATERMELON RIND PICKLES

This recipe comes from the vault of my husband's great-grandma Alice. It is a two-day recipe.

YIELD: **2 WECK** pint jars

Watermelon rind, peeled
1 cinnamon stick

OVERNIGHT SOAK:

¼ cup canning salt
3 cups water

BRINE:

1 cup (5 percent acidity) distilled white
  vinegar
1 cup water
1 cup sugar, organic or non-GMO
1 tsp. ground clove

Wash the skin of the watermelon, dry it off, and cut into quarters. Scrape away the pink juicy fruit, cleaning the pink flesh from the rind as well as possible. A spoon is a great tool to scrape with. Use a potato peeler to peel away the green tough outer layer of the watermelon. Once you have a prepped pale-colored rind, cut the watermelon rind into 1-inch strips and then again into 1-inch squares. Soak in salt water overnight.

The next day, rinse with cold water several times to remove the salt water from the rind. In a medium heavy-bottomed pot, heat the vinegar, water, sugar, and clove and bring to a boil. Boil 5 minutes, stirring frequently. Put the rinsed watermelon rind in a quart jar until it's full to 1 inch below the top of the jar. Fit the cinnamon stick in with the watermelon rind.

Ladle the hot brine over the rind. Use a funnel to safely transfer the brine to the jar. Leave ½ inch of headspace. Wipe the rim of the jar clean with a dampened lint-free towel or paper towel and again with a dry towel. Place a glass lid with rubber ring in place over the rim of each jar and carefully clip two metal clamps on each jar, one directly across from another. Process in the water bath for 10 minutes. Carefully remove the jars from the water bath with the canning tongs and place the jar on a towel for 12 hours without touching. Refrigerate after breaking the seal.

NOTES

PICKLED BEETS

After fermentation, the beets will become more tender but will retain a nice crunchiness.

YIELD: 1 WECK quart jar

6 small beets
2 whole star anises

BRINE:

1 tbsp. kosher salt,
dissolved in 2 cups water

Gently scrub beets clean of any dirt but do not peel. Trim the ends off and uniformly cut the beets into 1-inch chunks. Pack the beets into a WECK quart jar and cover with brine until they are completely submerged. Use a lid from a smaller WECK jar as a weight to hold the beet chunks underneath the brine.

Add the WECK jar ring and lid, and secure it shut by adding the metal clamps, one directly across from the other. Store at room temperature, ideally between 60 and 75°F (15 to 23°C).

This is a 2-week ferment. Be sure to check on the ferment every few days to make sure the brine remains over the beets and that no mold or yeast forms. If the brine is low, press the weight down to bring the brine back over the ferment. Once fermentation is complete, store in an airtight glass jar and refrigerate.

NOTES

FENNEL AND RADISH SLAW

This lovely colored pink slaw was a total experiment that turned into a favorite side to many meals in our household. The flavors meld together wonderfully.

YIELD: 1 WECK quart jar

1 fennel bulb, fronds removed, sliced

2 unpeeled watermelon radishes, thickly julienned

2 stalks celery, chopped

2 unpeeled carrots, grated

½ onion, thinly sliced

1 tbsp. kosher salt

Scrub the veggies and remove the ends and any bruised or damaged skins. There isn't a *right* way to chop up these vegetables, but the aforementioned notes are the way I prefer to chop them.

In a large, nonreactive bowl, mix the salt with the prepared veggies and pack them into a WECK quart jar, pushing down the mixture with your hands or a tamping tool. Within an hour, the natural liquid from the vegetables should release enough brine to cover the vegetables. If there is not enough brine to cover the vegetables, mix extra brine (1 tbsp. dissolved in 2 cups water) and add it to the jar until the vegetables are covered. Use a lid from a smaller WECK jar (or two, as needed) as a weight to hold the produce underneath the brine. Add the WECK jar ring and lid and secure it shut by adding the two metal clamps, one directly across from another. Ferment at room temperature, ideally between 60 to 75°F (15 to 23°C).

This is a 3-week ferment. Check on the ferment every few days to make sure the brine remains over the veggies and that no mold forms. If the brine is low, press down the weight to bring the brine back over the ferment. Once fermentation is complete, store in an airtight glass jar and refrigerate.

NOTES

CONVERSION CHARTS

METRIC AND IMPERIAL CONVERSIONS
(These conversions are rounded for convenience)

Ingredient	Cups/Tablespoons/Teaspoons	Ounces	Grams/Milliliters
Butter	1 cup = 16 tablespoons = 2 sticks	8 ounces	230 grams
Cheese, shredded	1 cup	4 ounces	110 grams
Cream cheese	1 tablespoon	0.5 ounce	14.5 grams
Cornstarch	1 tablespoon	0.3 ounce	8 grams
Flour, all-purpose	1 cup/1 tablespoon	4.5 ounces/0.3 ounce	125 grams/8 grams
Flour, whole wheat	1 cup	4 ounces	120 grams
Fruit, dried	1 cup	4 ounces	120 grams
Fruits or veggies, chopped	1 cup	5 to 7 ounces	145 to 200 grams
Fruits or veggies, pureed	1 cup	8.5 ounces	245 grams
Honey, maple syrup, or corn syrup	1 tablespoon	0.75 ounce	20 grams
Liquids: cream, milk, water, or juice	1 cup	8 fluid ounces	240 milliliters
Oats	1 cup	5.5 ounces	150 grams
Salt	1 teaspoon	0.2 ounce	6 grams
Spices: cinnamon, cloves, ginger, or nutmeg (ground)	1 teaspoon	0.2 ounce	5 milliliters
Sugar, brown, firmly packed	1 cup	7 ounces	200 grams
Sugar, white	1 cup/1 tablespoon	7 ounces/0.5 ounce	200 grams/12.5 grams
Vanilla extract	1 teaspoon	0.2 ounce	4 grams

OVEN TEMPERATURES

Fahrenheit	Celsius	Gas Mark
225°	110°	¼
250°	120°	½
275°	140°	1
300°	150°	2
325°	160°	3
350°	180°	4
375°	190°	5
400°	200°	6
425°	220°	7
450°	230°	8

INDEX

Pickled Mushrooms, 79
mustard seeds
Bread and Butter Pickles, 51
Green-Cherry-Tomato Sweet Relish, 67
Pickled Garlic-Dill Asparagus Spears, 75
Spicy Brussels Sprout Pickles, 52

N

nutmeg
Carrot Cake Jam, 56

O

onion powder
Bloody Mary Mix, 47
onions
Bread and Butter Pickles, 51
Brussels Sprout Kimchi, 124
Curtido, 108
Fiery Cider, 112
Fiery Cider Sauerkraut, 140
green
Jackfruit Kimchi, 123
Kimchi (Vegan-Friendly), 121–122
Green-Cherry-Tomato Sweet Relish, 67
Kimchi (Vegan-Friendly), 121–122
red
Cherry Salsa, 107
Cranberry-Apple Chutney, 60
Escabeche, 111
Papaya Chutney, 72
Pickled Red Onions, 130

Spicy Pear Chutney, 92
Strawberry Chutney, 147
Salsa, 133
white
Pickled Mushrooms, 79
orange juice
Cranberry-Apple Chutney, 60
Papaya Chutney, 72
oranges
Vodka, 162
Whiskey, 165
oregano
Curtido, 108
Diced Tomatoes, 64
Escabeche, 111
organic produce, 19–20

P

Papaya Chutney, 72
Parsnip Pickles, 126
peaches
Vodka, 162
Whiskey, 165
pears
Spicy Pear Chutney, 92
Whiskey, 165
peppercorns
Cauliflower and Beet Pickles, 55
Escabeche, 111
Pickled Mushrooms, 79
Pickled Red Onions, 130
Tequila, 170
Pickled Beets, 191

Pineapple
Pineapple-Mango
Pineapple-Strawberry
Strawberry
Vanilla Bean

W

water, 21, 31
Watermelon Rind Pickles, 189
WECK jars
  cylindrical, 16, 18
  deco, 16, 18
  history of, 13
  juice, 16
  mini mold, 17
  mold, 17, 18
  tulip, 17, 18
  weight, 31
Whiskey, 165

Apple-Cinnamon-Vanilla
Cherry
Cranberry
Orange-Clove-Cinnamon
Peach
Pear
Strawberry
Whole Raspberries in Light Syrup, 88
Worcestershire sauce
  Bloody Mary Mix, 47

Y

yeast. *See* Kahm yeast

Z

zucchini
  Pineapple Zucchini, 187

NOTES

NOTES

NOTES

NOTES

NOTES

NOTES

NOTES

NOTES

NOTES

NOTES

NOTES

NOTES

NOTES

NOTES

NOTES

ACKNOWLEDGMENTS

Thank you to my editor, Nicole Mele, and my publisher, Skyhorse Publishing, for proposing such a fantastic collaboration for a highly desired food preservation guide. Thank you to the WECK Company for choosing me to write this cookbook on behalf of your incredibly versatile and gorgeous jars.

Kindest regards to all my friends and family who are always enthusiastic about taste testing my experimental creations and offering invaluable feedback. I appreciate your support throughout my food-preservation journey.

Deep gratitude to my friends Kim and Aaron for letting me take over their kitchen, again.

A heartfelt thanks to my photographed friends ages 9 and under, for spending time with me and learning how to can and/or ferment.

A special thanks to all my guest contributors who shared a delicious canned or fermented recipe, designed from their heart. I'm honored to have each recipe included in this book. Gracious contributors: Emily Kociolek, Holly Howe, Illene Sofranko, Pam Lillis, Sarah Arrazola, Sue Ross DePaolo, and Wendy Jensen.

Finally, thank you to my husband and daughter that support me endlessly and deal with a ~~kitchen~~ house full of canned goods, fermenting jars/crocks of food, and infusions filling up every counter and shelf.